MW01289501

1957 EXPEDITIONS JOURNAL

*BAJA CALIFORNIA
AMERICAN MUSEUM OF NATURAL HISTORY
EXPEDITION JOURNAL SPRING 1957*

*HUAUTLA MEXICO
SEEKING THE SACRED MUSHROOM
WITH GORDON WASSON SUMMER 1957*

OAKES A. PLIMPTON

1957 Expeditions Journal
Baja California
American Museum of Natural History Expedition Journal Spring 1957
Huautla Mexico
Seeking The Sacred Mushroom With Gordon Wasson Summer 1957

Copyright © 2013, 2014 by Oakes A. Plimpton

All rights reserved. No part of this book may be used or reproduced by any means, graphic, electronic, or mechanical, including photocopying, recording, taping or by any information storage retrieval system without the written permission of the publisher except in the case of brief quotations embodied in critical articles and reviews.

iUniverse books may be ordered through booksellers or by contacting:

iUniverse LLC
1663 Liberty Drive
Bloomington, IN 47403
www.iuniverse.com
1-800-Authors (1-800-288-4677)

Because of the dynamic nature of the Internet, any web addresses or links contained in this book may have changed since publication and may no longer be valid. The views expressed in this work are solely those of the author and do not necessarily reflect the views of the publisher, and the publisher hereby disclaims any responsibility for them.

Any people depicted in stock imagery provided by Thinkstock are models, and such images are being used for illustrative purposes only.

Certain stock imagery © Thinkstock.

ISBN: 978-1-4759-8974-8 (sc)
ISBN: 978-1-4759-8973-1 (e)

Library of Congress Control Number: 2013908481

Printed in the United States of America

iUniverse rev. date: 08/21/2014

Contents

Illustrations—Photographs

Introduction

------◆------

everal years ago in the attic of my home in Arlington, Massachusetts, I came across the 1957 journal I had kept while on an American Museum of Natural History expedition to western Mexico. The Puritan expedition, as it came to be called for the schooner on which we sailed, visited islands on both coasts of Baja California as well as the Tres Marias islands to the south. I was charged with assisting four scientists, Curators at the Museum, each of whom has his own specialty.

In the journal, I also kept a diary of a subsequent trip in the summer of 1957 to Huautla, Mexico, with Gordon Wasson, to research the hallucinatory mushroom. Having learned touch-typing in the army, I transcribed both. I also found the slides I had taken of the expeditions and had them converted to Jpegs to illustrate the journals.

I graduated from Amherst College in June 1954, having majored in American studies. In those days, you were drafted into military service; the Korean War had just ended, and I was inducted into the army in October 1954. I served my two years as a radar operator at a Nike Guided Missile Site in Granite, Maryland (near Baltimore), also acting as a Clerk and Troop

Information & Education NCO showing off propaganda movies about communism in Eastern Europe, etcetera.

I was released from the army in October 1956, too late to apply for graduate school—what to do? I thought of pursuing my dream of going on a museum expedition, having grown up in New York where I had often visited the American Museum of Natural History. I applied. After first being told "no openings," about a month later I was called back and informed that the assistant to a planned expedition to Baja California couldn't go, so there was an opening. I applied and was accepted. I was to assist four scientists: William Emerson, collecting marine life, both current and fossil; Richard Van Gelder, collecting mammals; Richard Zweifel, collecting reptiles; and Donald Squires, who was to collect corals. The first page of the Puritan Expedition log further describes the purposes and personnel of the expedition.

Notes and Commentary follow both the Museum Expedition and the Mushroom Journals, with short biographies, expedition papers, published books by the principals, etc. Thanks to iUniverse Press for designing and helping me self-publish the manuscript. Two years ago, they helped me self-publish a journal I had kept of my year on a communal farm in New York State, entitled *1972 Farm Journal: A Back-to-the-Land Movement Story.*

Thanks especially to Richard Zweifel, for reviewing the manuscript and correcting more than a few misspellings of scientific names, as well as some grammatical errors and regular misspellings. Otherwise, I have resisted editing the original journal and have not excised critical comments or possibly politically incorrect language. Please pardon any excesses of my youthful writings—I was twenty-four.

Oakes Plimpton, April, 2013

Baja Expediton Journal

Explanation and Preparation

T his voyage on a hundred-foot schooner—all sponsored by a California millionaire who is some seventy-three years of age—is the result of my yearning for adventure. (I had imagined a safari into the depths of the Belgian Congo, but the museum informed me that native help is used nowadays.) This expedition will encompass the west coast of Lower California, the Tres Marias Islands, and the Gulf of California. We will be collecting marine invertebrates, coral, mammals and reptiles. I will be the scientific assistant to four scientists—all about thirty years of age—William Emerson, Donald Squires, Richard Van Gelder, and Richard Zweifel; they will be collecting marine invertebrates, corals, mammals, and reptiles, respectively.

I am not a scientist, although I have occasionally yearned to be one. They chose me from other applicants, as I am through with the army, presumably having some intelligence and a strong back, and as I am a mature and responsible individual—Ha! My function will be concerned mostly with the physical acts of collection and preparation (stuffing mice, for instance). The four scientists are interested in the following:

William Emerson, the leader, will be collecting marine invertebrates, especially Echinoderms, Brachiopods, and mollusks—looking for more complete data on their distribution than is already known (thermal data, particularly). He will also be interested in collecting fossil invertebrates—from the Pleistocene and Pliocene periods—for a more complete picture. The Gulf of California once supported a more tropical marine fauna, but in some of the shallow bays, especially on the west coast of Baja, some species exist that are next found in Panama going south.

Donald Squires will be looking for a coral reef, which he does not expect to find; should he find it, it would be the northernmost and (I think) the only reef off the west coast of a continent. Emerson is also interested in this, and is more confident of discovery.

Dick Van Gelder, mammalogist, will be interested in indigenous species of mice on the various islands that we will visit. He will also be after bats and rabbits, especially a rabbit on one of the islands that is coal black. Porpoises and seals will be another item on the agenda. We expect to collect porpoises with a crossbow!

Dick Zweifel, herpetologist, will be after indigenous reptiles on these islands. Informally, I offered to keep a list of the birds seen on the expedition, as that is my nature hobby.*

There have been quite a few other expeditions to these waters. Steinbeck went on one with Mr. Ricketts—the laboratory worker who appears throughout the pages of *Cannery Row* and *Sweet Thursday*—and the two wrote *Sea of Cortez* (another name for the Gulf of California). Steinbeck has a wonderful

---

* I couldn't find my list, but I did note all the birds I saw in the journal.

time describing the country, the Mexicans, the crew, the thrill of collecting, and his philosophical reveries while collecting and touring. The fauna hasn't been described thoroughly, however, by a long shot. I charted the exact locations of all the coral collections for Donald Squires, and there are many missing localities. Several of the islands have never been visited by either mammal or reptile collectors. The Tres Marias islands are comparatively virgin territory.

I spent most of January and February (1957) in the American Museum of Natural History preparing for the expedition. My duties consisted of sewing string onto one thousand mammal tags, tying five hundred reptile tags, putting together five dredges, tying nets together, and bolting the nets to the dredges. I was also responsible for general errands, such as packing equipment, shopping, etc. Furthermore, I swam at the YMCA under one Mac's direction—I was his replacement, as he couldn't go— swimming as many as sixty or more laps in a day, some with weights and a sweat suit on! Emerson, the marine biologist, could barely swim—thus the coaching. The four scientists' preparation was as thorough as might be imagined, especially Van Gelder, who card catalogued every item. In all, some fifteen large crates were sent—traps, ammunition, film, clothes, jars for collecting, alcohol, collecting cans, etc.

I also spent time locating coral collecting stations on the charts for Squires, typewriting descriptions of the islands for Van Gelder, writing down measurements of skunks for Van Gelder, and card cataloguing the Pleistocene and Pliocene mollusks, echinoderms, etc. of Baja California for Dr. Emerson. I drank coffee with the various curators, and found most of them to be rather engaging people, not at all the shy, retiring souls one would expect to find in a museum. I wandered through most of the museum doing my various jobs. They have, of course, a

3

terrific facility in size, if not in quality. To turn out an "Alaskan Brown Bear" took some $30,000 and hours of work! But the museum behind the scenes—the rows and rows of mammal skins and jars of reptiles dating right back to and before Teddy Roosevelt's elephant skins—is where the real work goes on. For instance, my sister Sarah's friend, Rufus Churcher, came to the museum to study red foxes. I shall express myself* with more vigor concerning the museum's activities after this trip is over.

---

* Couldn't find such expression.

Journey to Balboa, California
March 1–3, 1957

F ollowing a cocktail party at 1165,* the night of the thirty-first**—which brought together Dick Van Gelder, Dick Zweifel, all of my New York friends, some of George's (my brother) and some of Mother's—we set out for the west coast on a cold, snowy morning. The plane was first class (*not first class seating)* with an excellent lunch and cocktails before it, of which I did not partake. I divided my time between peering out the window at the Rockies and sleeping.

We arrived in Los Angeles at approximately four thirty in the afternoon, and then arrived in Balboa, our debarkation point, at six thirty. The schooner, *Puritan*, was easily found, and what an item of luxury it was! It was 102 feet long, 23 feet wide, gaff rigged, all white, and beautifully finished inside and out. Below could be found three single and one double bed rooms, and a large dining and drawing room combined, plus a cramped crew quarters forward, a galley, and the engine room. It was a yacht designed for protocol, for luxury, meant to

---

* 1165 Fifth Avenue, New York, entrance on Ninety-Eighth street. We lived on the fourteenth and fifteenth floors.
** Must have been the 28th (of February).

be immaculate, and not meant for the messy job of collecting animal life. Mr. Bauer, the owner, reputedly worth three hundred million dollars, was obviously not one who believed whole-heartedly in the Declaration of Independence or Roosevelt's New Deal, as there was a definite line of demarcation between the scientists and the crew. The steward served us, and although life was informal between the crew and us, when Mr. Bauer came aboard everything was very formal indeed. The Captain was very careful about not scratching the finish on the yacht, and even the deck was treated as though it were a dance floor. I tried hard to imagine what Mr. Bauer's feelings would be when Van Gelder dissected his porpoises on deck!

All of the crew seemed very much interested in the scientists' explorations. The two I knew best (Collins and Frank) were pleasant enough, but all too ready to boast of their prowess and ability as scientists—amateur, that is. And for that matter, everyone around here—including myself—talked altogether too much about their personal likes and dislikes of all the people involved in this trip. I hope this was the result of "reenlistment blues," and that all these petty grievances would be forgotten once the trip started.

I attempted surfboarding on Sunday without much success (getting out there was hard, twelve-year-olds passing me right by). A large California crowd was present, many poking around the rocky beach for shells, etc. Saw some Marbled Godwits *(large shorebirds)*.

Loading supplies, Don Squires at the helm

Expedition Begins—collecting
on islands ocean side of Baja

————◆◆◆————

March 4–6: Monday was spent further preparing for the trip, shopping, etc. Tuesday, likewise— loading the ship with provisions, food, etc. Monday brought several people by who had read the release in the newspapers, including one high school senior who left practically in tears when he was told he couldn't go. Tuesday, Mr. Bauer finally arrived, and we set sail around five in the evening. Mr. Bauer turns out to be a congenial old man whose main interest seems to be collections of shells. We eat like kings on this ship—our first meal was steak, baked potato with sour cream dressing, angel food cake, etc. Poor Dick Van Gelder got seasick and had to leave his steak untouched. Mr. Bauer spoke of his displeasure with Mr. Ricketts for identifying one mollusk as *Spondlyers* instead of *limbatus* Sowerby; he apparently didn't see that nature is not as well ordered as he would have it.

March 7–8: Our first taste of Mexico was Ensenada, where we checked through customs. It is a typically destitute Mexican town, no paved streets, etc. We have done all our "sailing" by power, and it doesn't look as though we will raise our sails at all. Our first taste of collecting occurred that afternoon off Todos Santos. We tried out the dredge in a hundred feet or so of water off the *Puritan*, and it succeeded! We found several *Murex* mollusks, aside from assorted starfish, anemones, and a few small fish. Great care was taken not to scrape the sides of the ship. The island itself is about half a mile long and a quarter mile wide, with a large rock essentially jutting out of the ocean. Zweifel collected several lizards and salamanders, while Van Gelder set his traps and put up the bat nets, the mesh fine enough so that the bats could not see or hear it. He tried to find a typical one-quarter acre to set his traps, so as to compare mice populations on the various islands, aside from other varying places—in all, over one hundred traps.

The next morning, we found only one *Peromyscus* (a genus of mouse), and nothing in the bat nets, save two white-crowned sparrows. We sat around in the evening armed to the teeth to shoot bats, but none appeared. The island is very green and lush, but nothing over two feet or so, thus probably the paucity of mice.

We spent the next day motoring through the fog to San Martin Island. Spent my time boning up on shells, and reading *Brave New World* (from the ship's library). Van Gelder slept so much that his self-winding watch stopped.

March 9: On San Martin Island I had my first taste of collecting reptiles—alligator and *Uta* lizards. The latter are similar to Florida chameleons, but the former are bigger and do bite, though without much effect. They are generally found under rocks in the coolness of the morning—though later, when warm, they can really move. A good number of sea lions were present, and we had the good fortune of seeing two adult and two baby killer whales cruise by several times, the young leaping high into the

Dredging! Van Gelder filming—chef,
captain, Squires, Emerson

air! Their dorsal fins stand some five feet, their black and white coloring heightening their sinister demeanor.

We saw numerous cormorants (Brandt's), gulls, pelicans, etc. No traps were set, and no dredging was in order, so we set out around noon for San Benito Islands, an all-night run. Took the wheel for about three hours, part of which was spent listening to Mr. Bauer spin yarns about his early prowess as a lawyer, and watching our herpetologist pickle his lizards. We had photographed them earlier. He first killed them by injecting them with Nembutal (if not already dead), slit them up the belly and down the tail, and then sat them in a formalin solution, before putting them to rest in alcohol.

The next day found us at one of the San Benito Islands—a mountainous, desert-like island of about a mile by half-mile (there are three islands in all). I again collected lizards, finding about ten to Zweifel's none, the reason being that I collected along the beach while he spent his time in the hills. Saw a rock wren, a horned lark, a song sparrow, four ospreys, two nests, and a few oystercatchers.

I also blundered onto some elephant seals—the males are great blubbery creatures with enormous proboscises, the females smaller, without the proboscis, but hardly elegant. When they moved (on land, that is), the males seemed to shake along by moving their flesh. The females seemed content to lie on their sides and snarl at any intrusion. The males had scars along their necks, evidencing what must have been pretty fierce battles. I saw two start a rather small scuffle, rising up and crashing against one another with sounds that issued from their very depths! Unfortunately, I didn't have a camera.

We went over to neighboring Cedros Island that afternoon, anchoring at South Bay. The island is very mountainous and bare. Dr. Emerson and I collected some Pleistocene shells; one could see a layer up to four feet thick of clamshells, and others overlaying a rocky shelf some twenty-five feet above sea level. There is a little fishing settlement on this part of the island, a little ramshackle group of filthy huts complete with women and tots.* I think I saw some Common Shearwaters on the trip from San Benito Islands.

March 10: A rather cold, windy day spent dredging South Bay in the small skiff. There is a motor driving a winch to pull up the dredge up an A-frame. We were moderately successful dredging great numbers of sand dollars, heart anemones, and only a few Gastropods including *Muria norrissii,* and an *Oliva.* Van Gelder caught eleven *Peromyscus,* while Zweifel shot about seven lizards.

March 11–12: Today we motored up to the northern section of Cedros Island, about a four-hour run. We picked a canyon about a half-mile wide at the start, fairly verdant in comparison to the barren, mountainous coastline. We spent the morning collecting fossils and lizards, right around the corner from South Bay. I picked Pleistocene fossils from a conglomerate layer overlaying a cliff face, some forty feet from the beach. After this sojourn, we continued up the East coast to the canyon mentioned before. Elephant tree cactus and other desert flora abound in this canyon, and—with a clear, blue sky and the hot afternoon sun—it presented a beautiful scene. Zweifel found a spotted night snake, collected for the first time on the island. I spent the afternoon shooting lizards with Van Gelder's pump gun using dust shot, mutilating some, and missing more.

---

* As I remember, their kitchen midden consisted largely of lobster shells. And we traded a whole bag of lobsters for a cartoon of cigarettes, two men coming out to our ship to barter. . . .

Collected coral; collected lizards

I shocked the dinner table by asking Mr. Bauer if his finest Rhine wine came from California, and I managed to elicit from him the statement that the Mexican government should tax the "filthy rich" to raise the standard of living and take care of the poor—all this after berating Roosevelt. He is one of those who blame the world's ills on FDR.

I lost three dollars playing poker with the crew. I enjoyed myself thoroughly, though Mr. Bauer couldn't see how anyone could have fun losing at poker.

The next morning I rose early to accompany Dick Van Gelder on his morning trap run. He had set out about seventy-five traps and collected about six *Peromyscus*, five *Perognathus*, and one wood rat. *Peromyscus* is a white-footed mouse, while *Perognathus* is slightly smaller, with cheek pouches for storing nuts. This was a cloudy morning, so I didn't get any decent photographs of the island.

From here we proceeded to motor to Turtle Bay, a six-hour trip. Along the way, I saw a hundred or more shearwaters, which, after some deliberation, I decided were Common Shearwaters, not Pink-footed. I was assigned to dredge with Fred the engineer, but we were blanked by a broken gas line in the outboard motor. The wind was kicking up quite a chop, and we were pretty much soaked, despite the short duration. Emerson, Zweifel and Van Gelder went ashore, almost capsizing in the process. Because of the wind, Zweifel found nary a lizard, and Emerson didn't find any fossils.

Santa Maria and Magdalena Bays

---◆◆◆---

March 13: Van Gelder got two *Peromyscus* out of forty traps, and we were off early, presumably to make the first collection of mammals and lizards on Ascension Island. But on arriving there, the reason was soon apparent, for the island was completely bare, with only the birds, presumably cormorants, to grace its shores. We then decided to make a run for Magdalena Bay—some twenty-four hours distant.

March 14: Spent some of the morning at the wheel, pounding through some ten foot swells, fortunately behind a thirty-knot breeze. Later in the morning, we saw some common dolphin—a porpoise brownish on top, and white underneath—playing about our ship. We arrived at Santa Maria Bay about one in the afternoon, just outside of Magdalena Bay.

I was immediately sent out to dredge with Fred and Di (a crew member). After we followed Di's suggestion to tie the chain (weighing some fifteen pounds) about fifteen feet up the rope from the dredge, we pulled up a whole bucketful of bottom—mostly mud. Before—and generally after—each dredge haul, I throw the lead to determine the depth, read off a thermometer for the bottom temperature, and sight through a lifeboat sextant to determine our position. This is done by turning the sextant horizontally and bringing together two known points (buoys, points of land, etc.) in order to measure the angle, and with a protractor, it is simple to figure out one's position.

Upon bringing all of this "bottom" to the ship, each dredge sample is individually put on a screen table arrangement, washed down, and sorted through for specimens—Gastropods, Echinoderms, etc. Then it is labeled, wrapped in cheesecloth, and put into a can with alcohol for preservation.

March 15: A sunny, blue day devoted mostly to dredging Santa Maria Bay. Results were huge pailsful of very fine sand, almost mud. Upon washing the sand away, there emerged; one piece of coral; several *Oliva* (a genus of snails); numerous sand dollars; crabs; olive snails—another genus of snails; and various small (half-inch or less) Gastropods, bivalves or Pelecypods *(a class of mollusks)*, many of them being juveniles. Emerson went tide pool collecting, finding some of the adults of the juveniles.

March 16: Saturday, no less … "Sailed" from Santa Maria Bay around the point into Magdalena Bay. We dredged off the *Puritan* some five hundred yards offshore without outstanding success—a rocky bottom. However on the third dredge haul we pulled up some five hundred red-clawed shrimp! We pulled into the bay opposite the seaport of Puerto Magdalena, a thriving community of ancient tumbledown shacks. Here we found a Pleistocene conglomerate, chock full of shells of all sorts. We spent the afternoon collecting these fossils—this conglomeration was located just off the beach. It had been collected before, save for the Echinoderms and corals. Saw Hudsonian Curlews, Willets, and several Heermann's Gulls trying unsuccessfully to steal fish from the pelicans, and hundreds of gulls flying and soaring some five hundred feet up and higher. Saw some sandpipers with pink and black bills that I was unable to identify.

March 17: Sunday—went dredging with Fred and spent most of the morning exploring a winding mangrove lagoon. Saw more of the curlews, which, on closer look, turn out to be Long-billed Curlews—their bills being almost the length of their bodies, and the cinnamon on the wings a good field mark. The Brown Pelicans down here have brilliant red pouches on their bills, contrasting with their bright, yellow heads. Also saw some Greater Yellowlegs, both kinds of egrets, a Louisiana Heron, a kingfisher, Semipalmated Plover, California Gulls, and some sandpeeps that I was unable to identify. The lagoon was reminiscent of the Everglades. On the way out, we tried to dig some clams, but without success. We also had to pull an *African Queen* scene to reach the bay, as the tide had receded.

After a lobster lunch we went way down the shore (with the skiff) some eight miles, making four dredge hauls, each one seeming heavier than the one before—one mud, another rocks, and two plain debris. For the third haul, we had to remove the outboard motor, and the fourth broke the weak link (designed so that if the dredge is stuck, one can pull it out sideways by breaking the four or five turns of marlin). We had to go ashore to handle it, filling six buckets, and the fourth remaining in the dredge. It took us an entire wet hour and a half to return. Night found us setting gopher traps, and attempting to run down a mouse.

March 18: Motored across the bay to Santa Margarita Island. Spent the afternoon tide pool collecting along the shore with Dr. Emerson.

March 19: Rain! Rained almost an inch—a rare occurrence in these parts.

Spent most of the day skin diving, collecting soft coral—brilliant yellow and purple branching from a rock base, and also some *Porites californica*, a hard coral that glows iridescent green under water. The rain set a new record for Magdalena Bay. We anchored opposite a naval station—everything very neat and orderly. Van Gelder had procured the Commander's assistance in catching bats.

March 20: Went down the beach with Dr. Emerson to collect fossils in the skiff. About two miles south of the *Puritan* along the beach, we noticed the beach to be black, and on closer look to be black with cormorants! For some two miles of the beach—to some half a mile out—was nothing but cormorants. We motored toward one point of land teeming with them, and so vast were their numbers—and so frantic and panicked their attempt to escape us—that the spray from the onrushing cormorants

Cormorants! Photo by Bill Emerson, AMNH Novitates 1894

soaked us! Several collided head on with the boat—most dove a split second before contact. Hardly any cormorants actually succeeded in getting airborne; one could have run down the beach and caught them. The shore was covered with guano, and the stench was quite noticeable. Having sent thousands of cormorants off, it seemed one could see long black lines of cormorants continuing on to infinity. There were at least two hundred thousand cormorants—probably as many as five hundred thousand—for if one counted fifty cormorants per foot of beach for ten thousand feet, you would have five hundred thousand! Great blue herons were mysteriously enjoying their company, some fifteen to twenty standing amongst them as if they were the commanders. Upon landing, we saw some Caracaras *(an eagle-like carrion hawk)*, and could walk to within fifteen feet of them. Black Turnstones, Heermann's Gull, Frigate Birds, Brown Pelicans, and others joined the throng. The cormorants were Brandt's.

We finally collected some fossils and headed for the ship. Mexican naval officers arrived to have lunch with us; I found that my Spanish was hardly sufficient to communicate. They seemed to be very nice men; Mr. Bauer and Van Gelder had a wonderful time trying out their Spanish with them.

We are now on the way to the Cape. Saw a whale—probably a humpback, but he was too far away to tell for sure.

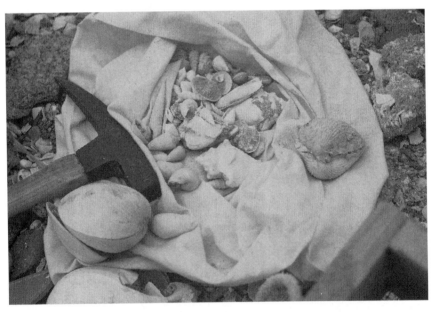

Fossils—Dr. Emerson collecting, shells collected.

Baja Cape and Tres Marias Islands

March 21: Motored all night and the next morning through a heavy swell, causing Dick Van Gelder to miss his second steak of the trip. We reached the Cape at noon. It is a beautiful day with the cliffs and bare mountains making a beautiful panorama. The water for the first time is crystal clear.

The town at the harbor is a typical Mexican affair, with the usual swarms of turkey vultures and dirty urchins. I collected herps with Zweifel, finding that my aim was not what it might have been with Van Gelder's pistol. The land is semiarid with cactus and mesquite-like bushes. All sorts of birds abounded, including the Hooded Oriole, Cardinal, Gila Woodpecker, Scrub Jay, and numerous others that I couldn't identify. Shot only three lizards—one of which hadn't been collected before—but I shot it up so badly, it is doubtful that Zweifel will keep it. Returned to the luxury of a bath (this was mainly a gasoline and watering stop). As of now, everyone's laundry is hanging from the rigging.

March 22: Spent all day motoring for the Tres Marias—even put up our sails to dry for a while. Saw my first albatross—

floating effortlessly over the waves, occasionally alighting, looking somewhat like a buoyant cardboard box. Besides our albatross (he was a Black-footed Albatross—all sooty, save for some white on his face and wings), there were myriads of Mother Carey's chickens, or petrels (Black and Leach's), and shearwaters seen. Sailed all night to reach the Tres Marias, only to spend a whole day and a half on the boat rocking like a cork in a stream, because our cautious Captain would not let us take the Lyman or the skiff in, claiming the surf was too high. It wasn't until Fred and I swam over to the nearest fishing boat—there were five of them in the bay—that we reached the shore.

Maria Madre Island is a penal colony, the prisoners having more or less the free run of the island. When we arrived they were about to start up a baseball game with the crews of the fishing boats in the bay. They apparently spend their time building boxes and domino sets. Van Gelder immediately started in, bargaining with them for mammals, reptiles, and shells. We left that evening with some five spiny-tailed iguana lizards—about one and a half feet in length, with their legs tied behind their backs by their tendons. They tried to sell us a seven-foot boa constrictor. Zweifel did purchase two four-foot boas for four dollars. Van Gelder also got two raccoon skins and a skull—the iguanas and raccoons are "steak" to these prisoners. There are a few Mexican-Americans there, apparently put away for two to three years for stealing cars. Some even have their families with them and have little plots of land and a hut to themselves.

After looking at a rather shell-less Pleistocene outcrop, and collecting some lizards along the beach, we were transported to the salt mines, some three miles distant. This was the winter season; thus, as the vegetation is tropical deciduous, there wasn't too much green. The forest was pretty thick, and apparently in the interior there were trees over a hundred feet high. The island is very hilly, with steep cliffs in many places dropping some three hundred feet into the sea.

I did not find out just how the salt mines operated, being more interested in a large flock of Black-necked Stilts cavorting about in an inland lagoon. We also saw a Tropical Parula Warbler and an Arizona Goldfinch—close by. A ground dove of undetermined variety abounded in the underbrush—there are some three species it could have been—different from Florida where a ground dove is a ground dove.

Tres Marias prisoners with some of the scientists

The next day was spent skin diving, with rather meager results, save for a staghorn coral and two varieties of *Porites*, a genus of coral. Found a *Strombus* (a genus of sea snails) along the beach and managed to find a *Murex* (another genus of sea snails) and a group of mollusks clustered into the coral. Also collected some lizards for Zweifel. Unfortunately had to endure the presence of Frank for most of the day.

Most of my skin diving was in murky waters, though later found some clearer water—complete with bilious green moray eels, green/purple lobsters, and a variety of tropical fish. Zweifel, Emerson, and Van Gelder returned from the hills with tales of Coppery-tailed Trogons, a beautiful king snake (somewhat resembling a coral snake), a vine snake—which is some five feet long and only about a half inch in circumference at its widest point—and also some fossil shells.

March 26: A dredging day. The load was so big that we had to beach it three times. As usual, mostly sand, rocks, and gravel were brought up, but on the sorting, several varieties of clam, a *Strombus*, and several small Gastropods were uncovered. I spent most of the afternoon dredging by myself, while Travers (Di) and Fred dove. Although Fred and Di came up with some large and rather spectacular shells, I managed to dredge up more than they did. I was bawled out for dredging alone, as were Fred and Di.

Went to the next island—about one and a half hours distant. Emerson bought some beautiful shells from the natives—I would love to find some alive. Collins and Van Gelder went ashore to set the traps, only to find the brush too thick to penetrate. After a veritable fusillade, they managed to return with two bats.

March 27: Spent the morning dredging and the afternoon skin diving. The skin diving occurred off a rocky beach in a panorama of fish, coral, sand, etc. One finds that in the effort of collecting, the beauty of the iridescent tropical fish and the color of the gorgonian or fan coral are hardly noticed. One could spend hours cruising through this underwater scene without ever losing interest. I saw my first shark—a long, graceful creature cruising ominously through the water. He came within about ten feet of me! I was retreating rapidly, shaking my iron at him (used for breaking off coral, etc.). But he turned away after a while; I would say it was about ten feet long—longer than me, at any rate.

I have forgotten to mention that Collins and Travers harpooned an all-black porpoise for Van Gelder in the morning. It apparently towed the skiff for some fifteen minutes before tiring. On returning later from dredging, Dick had had its head cut off and its belly cut open. He had tied the skull (which he kept) onto a log, and scores of hermit crabs were eating the flesh away. He also measured it, discovered it to be a male, and found that it had a tapeworm. He was unable to identify the species (of tapeworm).

That same morning, Collins, Travers, and Fred speared a manta ray, which towed the Lyman some seven miles at up to eight knots before they lost it. I also was fortunate enough to view a school of porpoise undulating through the water—almost comical to watch them move by an up and down movement of their bodies and to hear their high pitched squeaks—altogether different from the sounds of the shark.

March 28: Motored over to Maria Magdalena Island. Saw two whales (presumably finbacks) breach the surface some fifty yards from the ship, their great black bodies, flukes, and finally their tails emerging and submerging from the water.

We spent a rather futile afternoon dredging, netting two large Terebas (a spiral Gastropod), and only one *Oliva*. Our anchorage was poor, so we continued around the island for a more protected spot.

I have neglected to mention the early morning expedition to San Juanito Island with Van Gelder. We found twelve fruit bats, with wingspans of approximately one foot—in the bat net. We proceeded to rip great holes in the net, attempting to excavate the vicious creatures from the meshes of the net. We found two mice in the traps.

Sea turtle on the deck; the ship's outboard skiff

March 29: With picnic lunches, we journeyed forth into the bay to dredge—Travers, Fred and I. Very little luck—I think we netted three Gastropods and one hunk of coral out of seven dredges. Skin diving was equally unsuccessful, as the water was murky and the fauna rather sparse.

March 30: No dredging today. Went on a jaunt with Bill Emerson to collect fossils. We finally found a fossil belt some fifty feet or more near the top of a cliff. I clambered up to collect a rather meager collection of Pleistocene shells. Returned for lunch and a long afternoon nap. Di caught a turtle, and Van Gelder took some movies of Di dragging the turtle up to the swimming ladder and Zweifel taking it from him. Of course Di caught the turtle five hundred yards from the ship and had pulled it up onto the skiff.

At four o'clock Di, Fred, the two Dicks, and I left for a scramble up to a dry riverbed to some water where Zweifel had found a hitherto unknown frog (for this island) the day before. Van Gelder delivered an apt on-the-spot description of our venture *à la* the adventure writer: "The party hacked its way into the encroaching jungle, etc., etc." In fact, the dry riverbed served as an excellent path. The water consisted of only a few mud puddles, but there were a myriad of birds coming down to drink—robins, parula warblers, doves, cardinals, etc., and as the evening wore on the bats came down to drink and fill their tummies. I set up a line of traps on the high ground for Dick, though it looked devoid of mice. Along the riverbed, land crabs, in their shells, abounded.

When the bats emerged, we opened up on them (rifles with dust shot) with no luck on my part. Di shot three, and the bat net that we'd set up accounted for five or six more. No bats had been collected on this island before. I have neglected to mention

Myself collecting fossils 3/30, Emerson photo
1984 AMNH Novitates

that on the trip up, we captured quite a number of lizards. Dick Zweifel took the rectal temperatures of some of them. The vegetation near the water is much more luxuriant, with several huge fig trees dominating the scene.

March 31: We motored west some ten miles to a new anchorage, and a new water location. Dredging was the order of the day—and, for once, profitable. Though spectacular shells weren't present, the sorting turned up as many as a hundred shells per dredge—mostly small, spiral Gastropods—and quite a few new species for the islands.

April 1: April Fools' Day, which Van Gelder celebrated by playing straight cards, a rarity for him. There was more dredging, with less success —a few huge loads of dead coral. At four in the afternoon, I accompanied Dick Zweifel up a path and occasionally dry riverbed to the water on a bat-shooting, trap-setting, reptile-collecting expedition. The water again consisted of a few pools—but there were more of them, all situated in a somewhat spectacular canyon. At the head of the canyon is a 150-foot cliff face forming a horseshoe, down which trickled a minute stream of water. The birds would perch halfway up and drink their fill, the red of the Cardinal contrasting with the grey-green of the cliff in the evening light.

The bats started flying about five o'clock, and the two of us fired vast amounts of ammunition at the dodging creatures, mostly without effect. I finally shot one after some twelve shots, having to climb up a tree to retrieve it. While I was setting the traps, Zweifel shot six or seven. When it was too dark to shoot, we tried hitting the bats with sticks as they came down to drink. This is a fine sport far surpassing lawn baseball. I connected with seven or eight, only finding three as it was dark, the leaves camouflaging the stunned bats. Zweifel had better luck, belting his bats into another pool some seven feet from his batting stance and netting seven or eight. In all, we collected eighteen bats of five different species, much to Van Gelder's surprise and pleasure.[*]

A bat we collected—*dubiaquercus*? See footnote.

Upon sitting down for a picnic dinner, I suffered the ignominy of sitting down upon one of the rattraps I had set, which nipped me in the butt with some force. Although Zweifel found no frogs, he did uncover—while sifting through some dead leaves—an enormous boa constrictor, some seven feet long and weighing at least fifteen pounds. We had some trouble

---

[*] One of the bats turned out to be new to science, and Van Gelder named it after Zweifel and me—"doubtful oak"—*Bauerus dubiaquercus*. Zweifel means "doubt" in German (*dubia* in Latin) and "oak" is *quercus*. See http://scienceblogs. com/ tetrapodzoology/2011/04/11/antrozoins/.

getting the creature down the cliff (some twenty-five feet leading up to the horseshoe), and before we got him into the bag, he managed to nip me slightly with his needle sharp teeth (without much effect).

April 2: Hiked up to the water to collect trapped rodents. The total haul was two rats, about which Van Gelder could only mutter a few unmentionable words upon inspecting them, as they turned out to be the common Norway rat, not native to these islands.

Caught a fleeting glimpse of a trogon, which others had seen at close range.

On the way back, I managed to catch a five-foot indigo snake (with some trepidation) and later—with the indigo snake wrapped around one arm—a racer snake. Van Gelder took Mr. Bauer with him to another stream closer to the beach.

The rest of the morning was spent dredging from the *Puritan* en route to Maria Cleopha Island. We pulled up one very profitable haul from some twenty fathoms, and from thirty fathoms we pulled up an enormous haul, only to lose it as Frank let a coil loose from the winch, dropping the load three feet— just enough to break the weak link. That series of jolts tore the net, and the whole load—net and all—dropped into the sea.

Cleopha resembles the other islands with its rocky coast and generally drab vegetation, save the river valleys where huge fig trees grow.

April 3: Dredging scene again with very little success. Apparently, the bottom is rocky. We managed to pull up some crabs, which Emerson thought only resided on the beach. The dredging from the skiff was difficult as the outboard was not powerful enough to control either the speed or the direction. Often, the dredge will get stuck, and upon diving down to inspect the dredge in shallow water, it is usually caught only in a minor way. The other day we found that the weak link was stronger than the buoyancy of the skiff—as the green water poured over the stern before I stopped the winch motor, leaving Fred and Di yelling loudly! We weakened the link, though perhaps not sufficiently.

Mr. Bauer and company got on the subject of drunkenness at lunch. Van Gelder suggested that a drunk must be the skeleton in the closet in his family. He felt that Steinbeck wrote as he did because of his constant inebriation.

We will probably lose Frank at Mazatlán. He seems to have an enormous persecution complex. He is a punk seaman, unable to tie any knot correctly. He also has an inordinate fear of the unknown—hasn't gone near the water lately for fear of sharks, after all his talk of his eminence in the art of skin diving. Collins, at first sight a thoroughly objectionable drifter, turns out to be an excellent seaman, the only member of the crew who can handle the Lyman—beaching it, etc. And when one manages to get through his loud talking and nasty veneer, he's not a bad guy. Di, the other crewman, is thirty-seven, a big, husky man with the build of a professional football player. He doesn't have a job to speak of, this being a temporary gig. He is one of those who have exiled themselves from the complications of society, especially as concerns the eight-hour day and the conformities of being a "respectable" citizen. More about the crew later …

Emerson found more fossils along the beach, and Zweifel, armed with a newly sharpened machete, braved the underbrush to try to find a water hole. He was not successful in his venture, though there must be water somewhere on the island as a freshwater fish was reported here. There are no trails on the island, as on the others.

Dick Zweifel with racer, me with boa constrictor!

April 4: Spent the morning collecting fossils with Bill Emerson. The fossils were Pliocene—mostly *Pecten* (Scallops). Apparently *Pectens* have a wide geographic range but a narrow range in time, so that the age of a fossil bed can be determined by the species of *Pecten*. The fossils were embedded in the rock, requiring considerable effort to extract.

The afternoon was spent taking movies in the forest—movies of Zweifel recatching the seven-foot boa, catching an indigo snake (the one I caught), and a "live" shot of Zweifel catching a lizard. There were also shots of Zweifel and Van Gelder walking through the forest, Van Gelder chewing oatmeal and setting traps, and a Spiny-tailed iguana lizard. I found a path, though apparently not headed toward a spring or stream. Of course the movies came under the heading of "nature faking," but the reconstruction was fairly honest.

The dredge was finally repaired, and a new net was put on for the one that went for the deep six.

April 5: Dredged from the *Puritan* en route to Maria Madre Island, with considerable success. Huge loads were usual, with mud all over the deck—over a hundred shells in some loads—cones, *Murex*, etc. Emerson kept the sand and tiny shells to examine at the museum. The scientists are now at the Penal Colony bargaining for specimens.

April 6: Intended trip into the hinterland postponed until tomorrow. Spent the morning getting our boots shined and chasing some humpback whales in the Lyman. They were surfacing and leaping high into the air some five hundred yards from the *Puritan*, though when we took chase they ceased this bit, save for one great leap I managed to miss taking a picture of. I took about eight photos of their backs in bad light. The creatures were about thirty to thirty-five feet in length—we approached close enough to smell their stink.

The afternoon was spent bargaining at the salt mines for specimens. In all, we bought one lovely, green tree snake, one rabbit, some raccoon skins, one toad (which we had to buy twice, as it was stolen), and a multitude of shells. I saw the "Tres Marias Love Bird," a striking, iridescent, violet green parakeet, and at the Salt Lagoon I saw a Western Sandpiper, Black-necked Stilts, and Semipalmated Plovers.

April 7: Spent the morning waiting for transportation up to the Arroyo Hondo. There are two prisoners who have generally taken care of us—Tony, a Mexican-American, and Al (the same). Tony is the big operator, apparently there for stealing a car. Al is there for breaking someone's jaw and carving up the gendarmes with a broken bottle. Zweifel has given Al some materials for sending him specimens. There was one snake discovered here, a new species, which was lost in the mail, and no amphibians have been collected here. During the rainy season, frogs and amphibians abound; he should be rich.

The truck rumbled spasmodically to the arroyo, some fifteen kilometers distant. On the way, we saw some male Trogons—brilliant green on top, with a white throat and scarlet belly. At the arroyo, Emerson and I collected fossils along the beach, while Zweifel walked up the stream. Emerson and I were moderately successful, while Zweifel managed to collect a four-inch burrowing snake in a rotten log (a new record) and some fourteen tiny frogs of the same variety that he found on Magdalena. The stream at its upper reaches—it flows for about a mile ceasing some three miles from the beach—is apparently covered with rushes, save for an occasional pool where traps are set for doves when they come down to drink. The vegetation is very impressive—I managed to identify some Lark Sparrows drinking—hardly a spot for a desert sparrow. The birds abound—cardinals, ground doves, parula warblers being very common, as well as wrens, blue mockers, and a larger dove—rather few species, but great numbers of each. I managed to catch another racer, making nine all told for the islands, three or four of which were purchased.

More bargaining was done on our return to the Penal Colony— one long bargaining scene taking place with an ex-pawnbroker who managed to elicit ten pesos for a green tree snake, having wanted twenty.

April 8: Dredged off the *Puritan* opposite the mouth of Arroyo Hondo. We managed only three hauls—including one huge load of dead coral which, when sorted, included over a hundred shells, though mostly of one species. We then set the sails and actually sailed for two hours without the aid of the motor—an altogether pleasant scene not to hear the "coffee grinder." But the wind died, and for the afternoon we traveled under motor and sail for Isabel. We arrived there at four thirty. Isabel is a low volcanic island covered with Man-o'-war Birds, Brown Boobies (another type of seabird), Sooty Terns, Heermann's Gulls (a few), and twenty or so Red-billed Tropic Birds.

We went ashore, and I used up some ten pictures on the man-o'-war birds—thousands of them performing aerial acrobatics, the males puffing forth their red throats—nests, babies, eggs. I climbed one of the flimsy trees on which they nest. The great birds may perform brilliantly in the air, but on the ground they are very awkward, getting their wings caught in the branches trying to take off. I took about four pictures of one beautiful male with his pouch extended from some five feet out before he finally flew; one little chick was left on the nest clicking his bill and putting on a much braver show than his parent did.

Male Man-o'-war in breeding plumage—and in flight

Sooty terns close to us; Mr. Bauer amidst the tern colony

April 9: Spent the morning skin diving with Fred. Found no mollusks, but collected some five species of fan coral. Fred tried to spear some large sea bass or grouper with his gun, without success.

This afternoon Mr. Bauer, Dr. Emerson, the Captain, and I hiked over the island to the Sooty Tern rookery. In an area of some five acres or more, thousands of terns were nesting. The noise is so terrific when one walks through the nesting terns that one has to shout to be understood. The terns are brave creatures—flying at you, picking at your legs, and only leaving their egg or young upon greatest provocation. They build no nest, laying their egg on the bare ground. The nesting site is a rocky, treeless area. They lay only one egg—a few had hatched, the fledglings covered with brown down. I must have taken twenty pictures of these terns.

Mazatlán—Entering the Gulf of California

T omorrow—Mazatlán. Six days—a bad scene—six days, as we had to get the anchor winch repaired—put on water, fuel, etc. We said good-bye to Mr. Bauer and Frank—good riddance! Mazatlán has a pleasant seashore location, some decent modern architecture, a wide shore drive, and the usual squalor of a Mexican town. On the eleventh we saw Dick Zweifel off—half the crew and the rest of us drunkenly trooping out to the airport to see him off—much to his embarrassment. On the same day, we welcomed Don Squires and John Soule—a last minute acquisition who is an expert on Bryazoa, a microscopic moss animal that the uninitiated would mistake for algae.

I spent most of my time seeing the more sordid sections of town with Collins, Di, Fred, Van Gelder and Clyde. We spent considerable time at a striptease joint that had a very loud band and an absurd floor show that started that night at twelve thirty with one stripper who finally emerged around one fifteen. One night, Clyde, Van Gelder, and I were treated there to America in action, as well as to drinks for most of the evening. Our benefactor was a great, florid millionaire who sat babbling about the virtues of having guts. "God has guts—he's no meek man!" he said, while fondling the rising beauties of the "B" girl sitting beside him. We had originally been accompanied by Fred and Di—Fred with a newly purchased machete, and Di rapping the knife into the table at various intervals. Fred has been in the highest spirits this evening—emitting loud, apelike cries (hidden obscenities), and occasionally leaning over toward Clyde, shouting, "Shut up, you loud drunk!" When we returned at about three, we found Fred at our hotel (a very comfortable establishment, by the way), looking very subdued.

Di is in jail having torn apart a whorehouse on discovering himself conned of 250 pesos. The Mexican jail is merely a walled in courtyard—not even cemented—run by a fat slob. After two hours of brilliant defense by Van Gelder—trying to talk a taxi driver out of 50 pesos for a fictitious broken door handle, and trying to talk down a 500 peso fine and damages—we ended up paying 650 pesos.

Saw a very amateur bull fight. I spent parts of two days dredging and skin diving with Don Squires.

Left for Los Frailes, the end of Baja California, on the sixteenth. I took the eight-to-twelve and four-to-eight watches with Charlie *(during the day I think)*. Woke up to find my elbow all swollen, somewhat like housemaid's knee—only apparently infected. This prevented me from exploring Pulmo Reef with Don Squires and company, a much richer coral formation than anything we had come across before. It is not a constructional coral reef—the coral growth is luxuriant, but it doesn't seem to be growing on its own dead skeleton. Soule collected some herps for me—lizards. We also dredged off the *Puritan* with some success.

April 20: Steamed for Ceralbo Island. As my elbow has gone down somewhat and small fever has disappeared, I am let loose to set traps and shoot up the countryside. Shot ten lizards, walking seemingly endlessly up a canyon—usual arid vegetation—cactus, mesquite, etc. The crew harpooned another porpoise only to have the quarter-inch nylon line part.

April 21: (Easter Sunday) Left for Espiritu Santo Island, which we reached about two in the afternoon. This is a low island, and we anchored opposite a low, flat coastal plain approximately two miles wide and reaching as much as one mile inland. I went ashore to set traps and to shoot up the countryside for the endemic black rabbit and supposedly endemic ground squirrels. I managed to shoot three ground squirrels, but had no luck with the moving targets presented by the rabbits. We tried to "jack" the rabbits at night *('freeze' them by shining lights),* with no success either. Collected several lizards, but no rattlesnakes seen.

April 22: Steamed around to the Western side of Espiritu Santo to San Gabriel Bay, dredging on the way. Embarked at the shore for another séance with the rabbits and ground squirrels. Clyde came with us. After tramping up and down a red sandstone canyon for hours and shooting at numerous rabbits, I finally bagged one! Clyde also got one, literally blowing its head off. Spent half the afternoon running up the canyon walls after rabbits. Saw some Red Crossbills and a Ladder-backed Woodpecker. Also shot one ground squirrel.

Don found a true constructional coral reef (the live coral growing on top of the dead) the first such found on the gulf. All sorts of mollusks were found while we were skin diving, and even Emerson was found splashing about in the shallow water.

I skinned and stuffed a rat and a ground squirrel for the first time.

April 23: Steamed for La Paz to refuel and take on water. La Paz *(Spanish for "peace")* lives up to its name—very little of the commercialism and pace of Mazatlán. We stayed in tonight.

Prepared mouse skins; shot black rabbit.

Accident! Back to La Paz and then New York

---✦---

April 24: Steamed for the northern part of Espiritu Santo and anchored between Espiritu Santo Isla and Roca Partida (the two are almost connected by a sand spit).

I clambered ashore about eleven in the morning. Armed with a picnic lunch, traps, gun, pistol, etc. to shoot rabbits and ground squirrels. It was the same red sandstone here—same country as we encountered at San Gabriel Bay. I shot a rabbit, a ground squirrel, and about eight lizards before the bad scene occurred. I was pointing the pistol at a lizard, all cocked and ready to fire, when I noticed that the forward site had slipped toward the middle of the barrel. Pushing it forward, I somehow managed to put the end of my finger over the barrel and fire the pistol simultaneously, thus filling the end of my index finger full of dust shot, and in fact blowing a hole though it!

On the way back to the shore I shot another rabbit and some more lizards (denial!). I waved at Squires who was out in the skiff, dredging. He picked me up and we left for the *Puritan* about four o'clock. (I shot myself at one thirty). Everyone being aboard, we steamed for La Paz.

We managed to find a good German doctor who looked at my finger in the fluoroscope. You couldn't see the bone for the lead. He probed around with a pair of tweezers and gauze, running it on one side of the finger and out the other to remove the lead. When we left him at eight that night, he seemed pretty optimistic about it, but the next day found about half the pellets left. Operating while peering through the fluoroscope, he couldn't remove the rest as they were embedded in the flesh and bone. Thus, I have to go to New York!

Spent the afternoon drinking rum with the crew, Van Gelder, and Squires. Tomorrow at six in the morning I leave for Los Angeles and from there I go to New York. *Bad scene*!

April 26–May 4: My Uncle Cal is a doctor (Calvin Plimpton, M.D.) and he arranged to have my finger operated on by a surgeon who usually operates on hearts (!) at Presbyterian Hospital in New York. He removed the rest of the pellets and shattered bone; my finger would be bandaged for a while, but would be essentially okay (if ugly). *For instance, I can type with it (transcribing my journal here!).*

Return to the *Puritan* and the Sea of Cortez

M ay 5: Returned! Flew to Loreto and stayed one night at a fashionable sporting club. Set out in a fishing boat to find the *Puritan* and fortunately found it at Salinas Bay, Carmen Island. Great astonishment upon arrival! People glad to see me.

I should backtrack a little. Mr. Bauer has changed his mind, and the whole gulf is to be covered; the trip to Catalina Island is called off—so I was both messenger *(from the museum)* and again an assistant!

After I arrived, we motored to Punta Escondido Hidden Harbor on the mainland. We anchored in one protected harbor, and through a shoal opening lay another large harbor, five hundred or more yards across. On the mainland, the mountains rise abruptly to some 2,500 feet, barren mostly, save for an occasional green oasis. Set some traps on the mainland—same arid vegetation. Occasionally, the thorn bushes have rather exquisite red or pink blossoms. That night we went bat shooting, failing as usual to shoot any—I blasted away some eleven shots without even coming close. Squires had been taking my place setting traps, etc., as he usually finished with his coral collecting by the afternoon.

Apparently, the night before I arrived, everyone celebrated

the second month of the voyage with rum. As usual, Di and Collins lost their heads, and various altercations followed. The Captain lays down the law: no communication between crew and scientists, especially talking about their problems (personalities) with the crew. I doubt that this will be followed very closely, but it should be, and the dissension in the scientific ranks (which there is) ought to be soft-pedaled (which it isn't). Bill Emerson is not a leader. He is loath to show much enthusiasm, he doesn't care much for the physical act of collecting, and he hasn't the facility for making others enthusiastic about this trip, the crew especially. Don Squires, for instance, has the crew in the palm of his hand, naming new kinds of coral after them, and going at the collecting with great enthusiasm and drive. Soule is somewhat of a sore spot—he doesn't swim either, and he does even less field work than Emerson. There is bitterness at his presence in the first place, as he was a last-minute choice by Bill Emerson. *(Perhaps I should have followed my own advice—soft-pedaling criticism. I do remember enjoying collecting with him.)*

May 6: Left for Carmen Island. Found two *Peromyscus* and two *Perognathus* (deer mouse and pocket mouse) in my traps. Van Gelder got skunked. Spent the afternoon shooting lizards and setting traps (Van Gelder set his on a small neighboring island.) Emerson and Squires were looking over the fossil formations. The flies were plentiful.

Swam back to the *Puritan* with Don, holding my bandaged finger above the water, thus effectively having to swim with just my legs. The water was wonderfully refreshing. Took me about half an hour or more to swim the quarter mile out to the boat. Shot at bats again that evening and got skunked.

To backtrack a little, Van Gelder had better luck after I left, even winning a quarter from the Captain that he would catch more mice than the number of fish the Captain caught. The Captain got ten fish, but Dick trapped seventeen mice. He trapped fifty-five mice in three days.

May 7: Found three *Peromyscus*. Dick got one *Perognathus*. Sailed for Coronados Island. This island alternates between sand dunes, sand, coarse lava boulders extending for the greatest area, and finer lava boulders. Walked for hours amongst the boulders finding no lizards, but seeing some sort of warbler and some sparrows. Don, Dick, and I set traps, numbering some 120 in all. We only shot three lizards.

May 8: Got skunked on Coronados. Dick got one *Peromyscus*, a distinct species from the others we've been getting. Sailed for Ildefonso Island, a volcanic rock soaring out of the sea only about three-quarters of a mile long and a half-mile wide. We set 120 traps again, Don helping us, though I doubt there are many mice here. Ospreys, boobies, ravens, and man-o'-wars abound.

After the traps, we sailed for Pulpito Point for our anchorage and to collect coral. Put a rubber *(condom borrowed from the crew)* on my finger and swam with Don, finding one or two mollusks and a *Porites* coral. There is kelp here, and one can cruise down avenues of the stuff—large grouper, etc. are common.

May 9: Skunked on Ildefonso Island, save for one three-inch centipede *(caught in a trap)*. Caught a Sceloporus *(spiny lizard)* alive. Traveled to Santa Inez Island—no sign of mice; shot four lizards. San Marcos—a great hunk of barren country was next. Set traps and shot at one lizard and missed. Walked miles attempting to shoot bats, but saw none. There is a town on the island, palm trees, etc.

May 10: Picked up traps—one *Perognathus*. Dick got one rat, and Don, with sixty-three traps set, got one *Perognathus* with a crushed skull, therefore useless. Spent the morning shooting lizards, garnering three. Motor-sailed to Tortuga Island. Set traps and shot five lizards. Another lava island—I predict over five mice apiece, hopefully. As there is no anchorage here, we sail back to San Marcos. Went bat shooting there, but no bats.

I discovered from Don and Dick that I came close to meeting the *Puritan* at Loreto, as the Captain was ready to fire Di and Collins and attempt to pick up another crew. He called a general meeting at one in the morning to inform the scientists of his intention, but he was persuaded to wait until morning. The small "two-month anniversary party" apparently conformed to Steinbeck's analysis, being a jolly affair until Dick and Don left, at which point the "Hyde" side of Di shone forth.

When the Captain told them to shut up, they told him to go to hell. The Captain called it a mutiny! But by the time I arrived (the next morning) all seemed water over the dam, as nothing had changed since the Captain laid down the law about fraternization between the crew and us.

We had an amusing scene today—the *Puritan* rolled so far that Van Gelder tipped over in his chair and was sent sprawling to the deck, and Don received the silver drawer in his lap.

May 11: Great scene: found nine mice in my traps. Dick and Don both got fifteen! The *Puritan* raised sail, and we sat on the hill taking pictures from about eight cameras—more, in fact. Spent the rest of the day skinning mice.

Sailed for a while and then motor-sailed for San Carlos Bay, a beautiful spot completely surrounded by mountains—two resembling (and called) Goat Tit Mountains. Went ashore to put up the bat nets and shoot bats. Put them next to a pothole with water. By the time we left, there were some seven bats in the net, and we shot four or five, also a nightjar, probably a Common Poorwill, thinking it to be a large bat.

May 12: Went ashore with Clyde to find a chipmunk that was caught—and subsequently escaped—on an expedition which Zweifel was on a few years ago. Despite a great deal of tramping, we saw no sign of it. We did shoot about eight Cnemis *(whip-tailed lizards)* to fatten a series of two that Zweifel had collected before, and which is apparently a new species. Dick collected about twelve bats—five different species—several of which had apparently chewed their way out of the net.

After this interlude, we motored for Guaymas to refuel, etc. Guaymas is a typical, dusty Mexican town with its one large cathedral and set against a backdrop of barren mountains. It lacks the occasional modern architecture and ocean drives of Mazatlán. After an evening of cribbage, I was persuaded to go a-shore with Fred to pick up Collins, Di, and Sperry (the cook) from a night on the town. They were all waiting for us, surprisingly enough. Di trapped me into a philosophical conversation in which he bemoaned the evolution of society toward socialism—television, Red Cross, pensions, etc.—no more neighborly scenes—and he predicted our doom! His cardinal bit is not only to "know thyself" but also to "accept yourself." He threatens to send me his short stories, which from his synopses are a very gloomy lot—and wordy.

May 13: Refreshing day—also, John Soule left us. A good scientist, I gather, but Lord, what a personality. He calls me "Laddy" and calls everyone but Bill Emerson "Dad." He slurps his coffee from a crouched position, and then emits a great "Aah." And his conversational gambits are pitiful.

May 14: Motored to San Pedro Nolasco Island. A great rock jutting out of the ocean constitutes the island. As Dick was feeling badly, I was sent alone and found myself in a mountain climbing scene, the only possible entrance constituting a hundred-foot climb (or less), some of it difficult as the rock was rotten. I set about fifty traps—hurriedly, as we had yet an hour's sail to an anchorage. When the top level was finally reached, various cactuses and grasses were growing mostly on steep valleys, some in bloom—red and yellow flowers. I saw one large iguana, which I shot at from a distance of about ten feet with apparently no effect, as it scampered off under the rocks. There were crowds of boobies, Man-o'-wars, Heermann's Gulls, and pelicans fishing off the island. I also bumped into four baby pelicans up on the rock.

I went ashore at our anchorage to shoot bats (I didn't see one), the sun setting against a background of jagged bare peaks with cactus, chollas (a desert plant), etc. Saw a bevy of Desert Quail, pearl gray, with jaunty feathers adorning their crest and chestnut and white-striped sides.

May 15: Skunked again! When two kinds of mice are competing for one hunk of rock, there seem to be smaller populations (says Van Gelder). I shot seven lizards, including two iguanas and four different kinds.

Spent the day bucking a fifteen-to-twenty-knot northwest gale with motor and sail. Tiburon is our destination. We should reach it by midnight. We have had to tack, and as you can tell from the writing *(wobbly!)* there is considerable pitch and roll. Saw a Black-footed Albatross which is not reported here, also Black Petrels, Tropic Birds, shearwaters, boobies, etc.

May 16: We are at Tiburon Island, land of the Seri Indians—once the scourge of Sonora, and occasionally troublesome within the

Typical scenery—Twin Peaks,
Columnar cacti of the Sahuaro sort.

The Crew—Di Travers and Fred, the
Engineer; the *Puritan* under sail!

last fifty years. Went swimming with Don in the morning, finding very little—flocks of Royal Terns, pelicans, Heermann's Gulls, and boobies fishing alongside of us. We walked all over the island in the afternoon—same sort of country—washes and hills studded with cactus, scrubby trees, thorns, etc. I had only one noose on the end of a nine-foot pole with which to catch lizards—an impossible task with the wind. I finally stoned one to death. Jack rabbits were common here—think I could have shot five or six without any trouble. Don and Dick have gone off to trap at Turner's Island where there is a subspecies of *Perognathus* known by only one specimen.

We went ashore at night for an unsuccessful bat shoot, but had far better luck upon returning to the ship to gun for fish-eating bats. We rigged up a light and formed a veritable ack-ack battery with shotguns, a pistol, and a rifle—banging away at the bats, which to the surprise of everyone, appeared. These bats have strongly-hooked claws on their hind feet, with which they hook small fish when they are jumping or very close to the surface. We would all troop from one side of the boat to the other as Fred moved the searchlight. We shot nine in all. Don and I played retriever for awhile, until the Lyman was finally lowered. Don actually batted one down with his hand onto the water, and—amidst cheering—he leapt on top of it and caught it!

These bats are quite big, their wingspread being about eighteen inches. Their flight is not as erratic as the insectivorous bats, so they are not hard to shoot. Their range only includes the northern part of the gulf—Guaymas and Cedros Island.

May 17: Caught nineteen! Collected two *Peromyscus*, fifteen *Perognathus* (mostly young and ant-chewed), and two rats—from approximately fifty mousetraps and six rattraps. Almost all the traps were sprung, and I got three tails—two *Perognathus* and one rat. I also saw a coyote trotting along the hillside some five hundred yards distant.

A bad scene followed upon return as the engine gave out, and the day was spent stuffing our specimens and expecting any moment to set sail for Guaymas. For once there was no wind—if I have forgotten to mention it, we were originally and repeatedly told that the gulf would be like glass, but this was the first day thus. We waited all day expecting to go to Guaymas, but at the end of the day it turned out the engine was all right. An earlier backfire had apparently forced water through the system. So a day was wasted.

May 18: We dredged on the way to Esteban Island. I went ashore after lunch to shoot lizards and trap. Shot about twenty lizards including two enormous ones requiring about five loads of dust shot apiece. One was perched in a tree, and I mistook it for a bird. We tried bat shooting again off the *Puritan*—had movie cameras again—but only bagged one. I played retriever in the Lyman.

May 19: Skunked again, after predicting a large haul. Dick got two *Peromyscus*, Don got one, and one *Rattus rattus* (European brown rat—first such reported on this island). We then motored for South San Lorenzo Island. On the way, I pickled the lizards—including three more large creatures that I had shot in the morning. Went ashore as usual to shoot lizards, getting a rather slim haul. Both Di and Don captured big chuckwallas (large iguanas), one of which escaped and almost ran off the boat. The island is—as usual—mountainous with desert vegetation. Oystercatchers, Royal Terns, Double-crested Cormorants, Sooty Shearwaters, Heermann's Gulls, and Western Gulls abound. Also spied a Red-tailed Hawk circling with the Ospreys and some Eared Grebes and Ladder-backed Woodpeckers. Set my fifty traps and returned to the routine of cribbage, three-handed bridge for a change, and reading science fiction.

May 20: Caught ten mice and two tails, including four *Perognathus,* heretofore not recorded here. Don caught sixteen, Dick got four—in all, fourteen *Perognathus* and sixteen *Peromyscus.* Don even caught two *Peromyscus* in one rattrap. The morning was spent motoring for Angel de la Guarda Island (while we were stuffing mice). We set out traps there and sailed for Partita Island to collect the fish-eating bat. We found them under the rocks there. If you dug furiously at a spot where their squeaks were issuing forth, you could catch one, or if you came upon a nesting petrel—either of two types, a Least Petrel or a Black Petrel. One petrel vomited what looked like blood when disturbed. We caught some ten bats in this fashion, including two babies clinging to their mothers. They cling to the rocks, which are loosely piled up to a depth of three feet or so. I managed to drop a rock on my shot finger causing it to bleed again.

We also went bat shooting from the *Puritan*, finally bagging four with over twenty shots. They were flying much higher. I managed to lose our radar lamp, attempting to net a blinded petrel, which Don and I thought was a bat.

May 21: Northwester blowing hard—spray all over the ship. It took us two and a half hours or more to make what took one hour yesterday. Caught one lousy *Peromyscus*; Dick caught one, too, plus one *Perognathus*. We motor-sailed for the north end of Angel de la Guarda—about a ten-hour sail. Angel is another rugged island, some fifty miles long and maybe ten miles wide or less, with peaks over five thousand feet. Set traps from four thirty to six, in the still of the evening.

May 22: Sailed to San Luis Gonzales bay—dredging on the way. Caught only one mouse, a *Perognathus*, but with his skull cracked, thus no good. Don got two; Dick, who set traps on Major Island, got six. Spent the day stuffing mice and bats. We had trouble at Gonzales Bay finding a small island on which two *Peromyscus* were supposed to have been found. Apparently, this has ceased to be an island since 1931 when a *Peromyscus* was last trapped, so Dick set his traps for one possibility and I on the other. "My island" connected to the mainland by a sand spit, only a pile of rock, and it would have been a miracle if I had caught any mice. I went fishing after supper with the Captain and Sperry, the cook. I caught three bass-like fish, two to five pounds approximately, while Sperry hooked a needlefish in the back, and the Captain caught a baby Bonita.

May 23: Miracles do happen. I set fourteen mousetraps, including two on the top of this rock, and caught nine *Peromyscus*. One trap was perched on the very top of the rock, an area about ten by ten feet, and it had a mouse in it. The others were just put down casually on the sand—since there were no bushes I could hide them under. Dick caught one of a different species from mine; thus we do not know if we trapped on the "island" described in 1931, as at that time two different species of *Peromyscus* were caught. Spent the morning stuffing these mice and the afternoon dredging. I lost two dollars on a ploy by Van Gelder and Squires, namely that a pound of feathers weighs more than a pound of gold, which it does! Practically rammed a finback whale, which breached not more than twenty feet from the bow of the ship.

San Luis Island is a "bird island," and I hesitantly submit that we won't catch any mice here. Reddish Egrets, Black-crowned Night Herons, Pelicans, Western Gulls, and Oystercatchers are all nesting here. About five thousand or more Double-crested

Cormorants were seen, and some Long-billed Curlews were on the mud flats.

We are presently packing up, for the end of the trip is at hand. The day after tomorrow we reach San Felipe.

May 24: Wrong again, for I caught one European rat and five European mice. Took some pictures of baby pelicans, cormorants, etc. The day was spent sailing for San Felipe, the skipper prohibiting the use of alcohol for the last night—but it was still a gay affair. I engaged in a pie-throwing contest with Don, and we played Hearts until about midnight. We had spent most of the day packing and stenciling the boxes.

Southwest Research Station, Summary

M ay 25: Left for Los Angeles! We stayed overnight with Dick's aunt and flew the next day to the American Museum of Natural History's Southwest Research Station in Portal, Arizona. My sister, Sarah, spent the summer interning there. I discovered at the Douglas airport that I had been accepted into Harvard Law School. The research station is up in the mountains—wonderful weather and beautiful scenery. Dick, Sarah, and I drove up to the spruce-fir zone, country identical to that of Wyoming. Don Squires and I went for a morning ride, getting lost, etc.

I don't like summaries much, but the trip can surely be called an outstanding success—from Don Squire's and Dick Zweifel's viewpoints, but only a limited success from Van Gelder's. I'm not sure how successful Emerson feels it was. Dick planned to trap at least fifteen mice on each island (or thirty, if two different species), but only on a few islands did he reach such a figure. And on a number of islands he got skunked—or virtually skunked. We all pulled for him, but he doesn't have the resiliency of Don, and at times he became very hard to get along with, though perhaps his seasickness had something to do with it.

I find upon returning that I am to write up my birds; I will attempt to follow Dean Amadon's "Observations on Mexican Birds," (published in the *The Condor* in the March-April 1955 issue), but this will have to wait until I return from Cuernavaca (summer magic mushroom trip!).

My photographs are fair to good. I have one photo of the mountains and desert shrubbery at Hidden Harbor into which a hummingbird flew (the cover). Zweifel's were the best, with some wonderful close-ups of desert flowers.

Dick Van Gelder and Vera are engaged and will be married some time in October. It looks as though Vera is going to be trapping mice on her honeymoon.

Well, turn the page for more adventures!

Note: I did write up a list of birds seen, but could not find it—all mentioned in the text anyway. Before the mushroom trip diary, turn the page for short biographies of the scientists and the author, and a list of the Puritan Expedition "papers" along with a map of Baja with the collecting stations listed.

Further note: A number of people, myself included, were surprised at the apparently readily accepted killing of wildlife for collection purposes— all those mice and lizards, and larger animals too such as the fish-eating bats, the black rabbits, the harpooned dolphin. As a scientific assistant back then, I never gave it a second thought. Yes, science—you need to have exact measurements and statistics. As Richard Zweifel wrote me (10/30/13) the new bat named after us could not have been described, nor the new genus discovered, without the bat in hand! The museum collections serve as repositories of specimens which are made available to responsible persons, comparable to libraries for books. "Collecting has to be done within reason, both with respect for need (does the museum already have a lot of material from a given area?) and population status of the target animals."

Notes and Commentary

The Puritan Expedition produced a number of scientific papers, listed following. First the conclusion of an article by Ass't Curator William K. Emerson "Results of the Puritan-American A.M.N.H. Expedition to Western Mexico, General Account," American Museum *Novitates # 1894, July 22, 1958.* Turn page for map and listing of collecting stations.

SUMMARY

The "Puritan" left Newport, California, on March 5 and returned after logging 4032 miles, on June 6, 1957. During this three-month period, 50 different collecting localities were visited, with the result that 183 marine stations, 31 fossil invertebrate stations, and 81 sediment stations were established. In addition to the large collections of recent and fossil invertebrates procured, more than 450 mammal specimens and over 400 herpetoligical specimens were taken.

The success of the expedition is largely due to the generosity of Mr. Harry J. Bauer, the excellent cooperation of Captain Anglesten and the members of the crew, and the kind cooperation of the officials of the Government of Mexico. The members of the scientific party are particuarlrly indebted to Mr. Oakes A. Plimpton for his invaluable assistance.[*]

---

[*] Appreciated! Accompanying the expedition was an experience of a lifetime! O.P.

Collecting Stations

1. Todos Santos Bay. 2. Todos Santos Islands. 3. San Martin Island. 4. West San Benito Island. 5. South Bay, Cedros Island. 6. Village, Cedros Island. 7. Lighthouse, Cedros Island. 8. Turtle Bay. 9. Santa Maria Bay. 10. Peurto Magdalena & Island. 11. Santa Margarita Island. 12. San Lucas Bay. 13. Maria Madre Island 14. San Juanito Island 15. Maria Magdalena Island 16. Maria Cleofas Island 17. Isabel Island. 18. Mazatlan. 19. Los Frailes Bay. 20. Ceralvo Island.21. Espiritu Santo Island (SE side). 22. San Gabriel Bay. 23. La Paz. 24. Isla Partida.25. San Francisco Island. 26. Amortajada Bay (San José Island). 29. Aqua Verda Bay. 30. Monserrate Island. 31 Santa Catalina Island. 32. Salinas Bay, Carmen Island. 33. Puerto Escondido. 33. Puerto Escondido (Danzante Island). 34. Marquer Bay (Carmen Island). 35. Coronados Island. 36. Pulpito Point. 37. Ildefonso Island. 38. Santa Inez Island. 39. San Marcos Island. 40. Tortuga Island. 41. San Carlos Bay. 42. Guaymas 43. San Pedro Bay (Nolasco Island). 44. Tiburon Island. 45. San Esteban Island. 46. South San Lorenzo Island. 47. Angel de la Guarda Island (SE tip, Partida Island). 48. Puerto Refugio, Angel de la Guarda Island. 49. Gonzaga Bay. 50. San Luis Island. 51. San Felipe

Note: If you google some of the collecting locations listed following, some have been developed as resorts. But such organizations as The Nature Conservancy and Conservation International are working to set aside Western Mexico islands as nature preserves, also to eradicate introduced species destructive of native species. Regards the procedures of our expedition, I am told that collecting now-a-days is less extensive, research more focused on animal behavior, suitable habitat, environmental considerations.

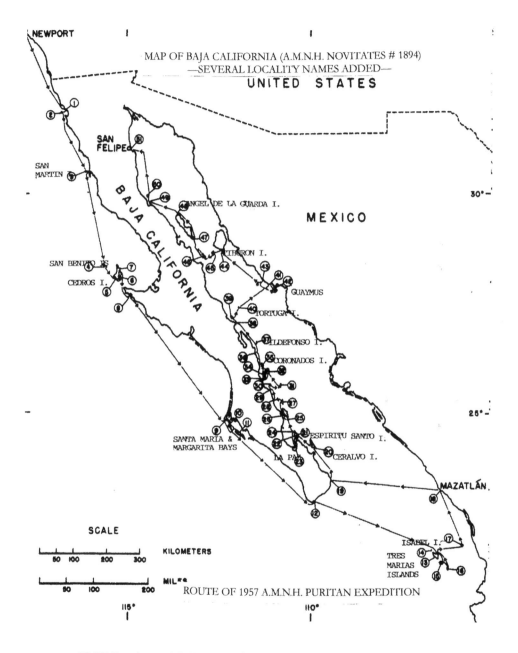

NEWPORT

MAP OF BAJA CALIFORNIA (A.M.N.H. NOVITATES # 1894)
—SEVERAL LOCALITY NAMES ADDED—
UNITED STATES

SAN
FELIPE

SAN
MARTIN

MEXICO

30°

BAJA CALIFORNIA

ANGEL DE LA GUARDA I.

TIBURON I.

SAN BENITO IS.

CEDROS I.

GUAYMUS

PORTUGA I.

ILDEFONSO I.

CORONADOS I.

25°

SANTA MARIA &
MARGARITA BAYS

ESPIRITU SANTO I.

CERALVO I.

LA PAZ

MAZATLÁN

SCALE

KILOMETERS

ISABEL I.

TRES
MARIAS
ISLANDS

50   100   200   300

MILES

50   100   200

ROUTE OF 1957 A.M.N.H. PURITAN EXPEDITION

115°   110°

1957 Puritan AMNH Baja California Expedition Map

Puritan Papers

1. William Emerson: *General Account* Amer. Mus. Novitates, 1958 #1894, pp 1-25. **2.** Richard G. Zweifel: *Notes on reptiles and amphibians from the Pacific coastal islands of Baja California.* Amer. Mus. Novitates, 1958, # 1895, pp 1-17. **3.** Leo G. Hertlein and William K. Emerson: *Pliocene and Pleistocene megafossils from the Tres Marias Islands.* Amer. Mus. Novitates, 1959, no. 1940, pp 1-15. **4.** John D. Soule: *Anascan Cheilostomata (Bryozoa) of the Gulf of California.* Amer. Mus. Novitates, 1959, # 1969,, pp. 1-54. **5.** Donald F. Squires: *Corals and coral reefs in the Gulf of California.* Bull. Amer. Nat. Hist. 1959, vol. 118, pp 367-432. **6.** Richard G. Van Gelder: *A new Antrozous (Mammalia, Vespertilionidae) from the Tres Marias Islands, Nayarit, Mexico.* Amer. Mus. Novitates, 1959, #1973, pp 1-14. **7.** Richard G. Zweifel: *Herpetology of the Tres Marias Islands.* Bull. Amer. Mus. Nat. Hist. 1960, vol 119, pp 77-128. **8.** Richard G. Van Gelder: *Marine mammals from the coasts of Baja California and the Tres Marias Islands, Mexico.* Amer. Mus. Novitates, 1960, # 1992, pp 1 - 27. **9.** William K. Emerson: *Pleistocene invertebrates from Ceralvo Island.* Amer. Mus. Novitates, 1960, # 1995, pp 1-6. *Shell middens of San Jose Island.* Ibid, #2013, pp 1-9. **10.** John D. Soule: *Ascophoran Cheilostamata (Bryozoa) of the Gulf of California.* Amer. Mus. Novitates, 1961, #2053, pp 1-66. **12.** William K. Emerson and William E. Old, Jr.: *The recent molluscs: Gastropoda, Cypraeacea.* 1962 #2112, pp 1-44. Ibid 1963, #2136, pp 1-32. The recent molluscs, Gastropoda, Strombacea, Tonnacea and Cymatiacea, 1963, #2153, pp 1-38. **13.** John D. Soule: *Cyclostomata, Ctenostomata (Ectoprocta), and Entoprocta of the Gulf of California.* Amer. Mus. Novitates, 1963, #2153, pp 1-38. **14.** William K. Emerson: *Results of the Puritan A.M.N.H. Expedition to Western Mexico The Recent Mollusks: Gastropoda: Harpidae, Vasidae, and Volutidae.* Amer. Mus. Novitates 1964 #2202, pp. 1-23.

Brief scientist biogaphies and publications

<u>William Keith Emerson</u>, Ph.D. U. C. Berkeley, is a malacologist, a biologist who studies mollusks. He is currently a Curator Emeritus at the American Museum of Natural History in New York City where he has been a curator since 1955. He was also Chairman of the Department of Living Invertebrates and head of the Malacology section for several decades.

Emerson has written 150 scientific publications and eight popular shell books including: *The American Museum of Natural History Guide to Shells: Land, Freshwater, and Marine from Nova Scotia to Florida* by William K. Emerson and Morris K. Jacobson, 1976, Alfred A. Knopf; *Shells* by William K. Emerson, Andreas Feininger, Hardcover, Thames and Hudson; *Shells from Cape Cod to Cape May: With Special Reference to the New York City Area* by Morris K. Jacobson, William K. Emerson, Softcover, Dover Publ; *Wonders of Barnacles* by William K. Emerson, Arnold Ross, Hardcover, Dodd, Mead; *Wonders of the World of Shells: Sea, Land, and Fresh-Water* by Morris K. Jacobson, William K. Emerson, Hardcover, Dodd, Mead.

<u>Richard George Van Gelder</u> (December 17, 1928 – February 23, 1994) was a prominent mammalogist who served as the Curator of Mammalogy for the American Museum of Natural History in New York for more than twenty-five years. Among his accomplishments at the Museum of Natural History was the 1969 redesign of the Hall of Ocean Life featuring the blue whale which still hangs in the center of the hall. In the late 1950s, while on the Puritan Expedition to the Baja Peninsula, he discovered a new species of vesper bat commonly known as Van Gelder's Bat *(see footnote April 1, 1957!)*. His later research included the

study of the nyala in Mozambique. He was a President of the American Society of Mammalogists.

He was the author of a number of mammalogy books including *Biology of Mammals* and *Mammals of the National Parks* as well as a large range of mammal related children's books such as *Bats, Animals in Winter, The Professor and the Mysterious Box, The Professor and the Vanishing Flags, Monkeys and Apes,* and *Whose Nose Is This?*

<u>Richard G. Zweifel</u> received his PhD at the University of California Berkeley in 1954 and was appointed Associate Curator in the Department of Amphibians and Reptiles at the American Museum of Natural History, New York City, shortly thereafter. He remained with the Museum serving at Associate Curator and then Curator until his retirement, having been Chairman of the (renamed) Department of Herpetology for one 10 year stretch. His duties at the Museum included supervising scientific aspects of the planned and constructed Hall of Reptiles and Amphibians, as well as extensive field work at home and away. He and wife Frances, a Scientific Illustrator who met at the Museum in 1956, retired to southern Arizona in 1989.

Bibliography: *Ecology, distribution and systematics of frogs of the Rana boylei group,* by Richard G. Zweifel, 1955; *Australian Frogs of the Family Microhylidae,* 1985. *Encyclopedia of Reptiles & Amphibians* (with Harold George Cogger and David Kirshner), 1998; *Encyclopedia of Animals: Mammals, Birds, Reptiles, Amphibians* (with Harold George Cogger, Joseph Forshaw, Edwin Gould and George Mckay).

<u>Donald F. Squires</u> - Prof. Emeritus of Marine Sciences at Connecicut University, was Director of the New York Sea Grant Institute. Author of *The Ocean Dumping Quandary — Waste*

Disposal in the New York Bight June 1983. Now resides in Tasmania!

Oakes Ames Plimpton — published books:
* *Prose Poetry* — with photographs - Swifty Printing, Arlington, 2012.
* *1975 Church Fire / 1981 Modern Design Replacement* Swifty Printing, Arlington, 2012.
* *1972 Farm Journal (Willet) — a Back-To-Land-Movement Story,* iUniverse Press, 2011.
* *Butler Ames and the Villa Balbianello, Lake Como.* Edited, Hobblebush Books, 2009.
* *Orchids at Christmas* by Oakes & Blanche Ames Etchings & Poems, Edited, 2007.
* *Robbins Farm Park, Arlington, Mass., A Local History from 1737-2007,* Penobscot Press
* *Stories of Early 20th Century Life, Compiled from Town Oral History* Edited, P.P. 1992

Notes: Oakes and Blanche Ames were my grandparents, Butler Ames my great uncle. I did go on to Harvard Law School, graduating in 1960. I worked for a number of years in anti-poverty law, but then switched to conservation — Legal Assistant at The Nature Conservancy from 1965 to 1968, graduate study in Environmental Planning at U/Mass Amherst 1969, Ass't Director of the Conservation Law Foundation from 1969 to 1971. I dropped out to spend a year on a communal organic farm in Willet, New York, self-publishing a book about the experience *1972 Farm Journal, a Back-to-the-Land Movement Story.*

Since then I have had volunteer jobs managing farmers'

markets — Somerville and Cambridge, then Arlington, coordinating volunteers for Nesenkeag Cooperative Farm, then started Waltham Fields Community Farm in 1995, and more recently a farm gleaning project — Boston Area Gleaners in 2004. Now, aside from occasional gardening and gleaning, I am retired to writing books, becoming 80 years old January 16th, 2013.

I'm married to Pat Magee (we go birding), have one son, Robin Plimpton-Magee, and live in Arlington, Massachusetts.

Turn page for summer Wasson Mushroom Trip, 1957 Journal.

ADDENDUM

After the publication date, I did receive a message from Don Squires. He's serving as an honorary Curator of Palaeontology (an original interest) at the Tasmanian Museum & Art Gallery. "Some years after the Puritan Expedition, I met John Steinbeck in a wonderfully interesting week in the Bahamas. Enjoyed telling stories with him re Sea of Cortez. He was actually pleased that someone had read his version of the Sea and utilized information therein to benefit . . . ."

I should add this story from the response by Dick Van Gelder's son Gordon: 'Incidentally, I met your brother George at (this) conference. "Does your brother have an injury to his finger?" I asked him*. "Yes," he replied, "It still flops a little".—"My father helped sew up that finger after it was shot."—"Hooray for Van Gelder!" said your brother.' * See pp 44, 45.

Mushroom Expedition Journal

Explanation, Setting Forth

———◆◆◆———

G ordon Wasson, a banker with J.P. Morgan, but also a
writer and an amateur anthropologist — essentially
the discoverer of the hallucinatory mushroom rite —
invited me to go along with his daughter Masha, friend Joan
Ferrante (school classmates of my sister, Sarah), and Valentina
Wasson, Md, a pediatritian and Gordon Wasson's wife, to help
out and share the experience. What follows is the journal I
kept!

This voyage mostly concerns hallucinatory mushrooms that
are eaten in a religious rite in an obscure Indian[*] village named
Huautla, in the hills of central Mexico. We also visited other
Indian towns to inquire about their mushroom rites, traveling
there by small planes and mules—no roads!

Laden with tape recording machines and the various
heavy luggage of the party, I set off in the family's 1954
Ford convertible—alone—for Mexico. Alan Richardson, the

———————————

[*]   Native American — Indian was the word then, and as noted
in the introduction I was 24 years old; I did not try to edit
according to today's standards.

Wasson's photographer, was originally going with me, but he dropped out. My average mileage was five hundred miles a day (there were no interstates back then).

My first stop was Roanoke, Virginia, and the second was Nashville, Tennessee, where I stayed at the Davis's house (uncle and aunt), which was occupied at the time by their cousins on the Davis side. He was the Dean of Freshmen at Yale; we spent our time discussing colleges, etc. The third night was spent in a motel near Texarkana, a town on the border of Arkansas and Texas. I spent the fourth night—July 4th—with United States Air Force Lieutenant Peter Crisp, watching a fireworks display and the panorama of Texas. The fifth night was spent in Loredo, Texas—on the Mexican border. I spent an afternoon arguing with the border guards and had to wire the Wassons for money to pay a new and very exorbitant tariff on the tape recorders, $130 in all. I unpacked the trunk completely four times, including twice on the Mexican side, once on the American side and once at an inspection station ten miles inside Mexico!

Cuernavaca—Dwight Morrow's House

———◆◆◆———

L eaving at six o'clock on a Saturday night, I drove straight through to Cuernavaca where the Wassons were staying—save for a two-and-a-half hour catnap in the car. Sunday is a banner day in Mexico—families mysteriously walk along the side of the road in the middle of nowhere apparently waiting for a bus. I asked one such family if I was on the right road for Mexico City and ended up taking the whole family to their destination—the parents and two cute little boys in front and their daughter sitting on top of a pile of inspected clothes in back. Great crowds were congregating in the towns all dressed in their Sunday best. I finally reached Cuernavaca at about four in the afternoon.

The Wassons were living in Dwight Morrow's house (once the ambassador to Mexico), a charming place partly because of its location smack in the middle of a tourist city. One enters off the noisy street into a spreading "villa" with three gardens, a lawn, and a lovely swimming pool—one imagines oneself in the country. The rooms were decorated with Mexican serapes; the servants were rather ancient and doted on the Morrows, who hadn't been there for twenty years, no doubt comparing Joanie

Ferrante and Masha Wasson with the Morrow girls and me with Lindbergh.

We spent our first week seeing the town—the teeming market place, etc., swimming, loafing, seeing some of Mexico City, especially the museum about the Aztecs and Mayans, including a representation of the sacrifice rite, some wonderful Mayan frescoes depicting war, Gods, etc., and a tomb. Mexico City has great numbers of modern glass and steel buildings, and a rather sorry imitation of the Empire State Building. The super highway to Cuernavaca, one of the few in Mexico, goes right by the university—the buildings all covered with Aztec-like frescoes swearing with the dull, cluttered landscape.

We also drove to Taxco, a silver mining town built on a hill, with all the houses dating back to the seventeenth century, or if not, built in that style. The countryside is very mountainous, and the red roofed village—with its cathedral with a brilliant tile dome—makes a beautiful scene. They also sold silver rather cheap, and I bought quite a few wedding presents.

Cuernavaca Market — Valentina Wasson,
Masha Wasson, Joanie Ferrante

Journey to Huautla

———◆———

F riday was the great day that we set out for our Indian
village and the mushroom. We set forth for Tehuacán,
stopping at various places on the way. At the town of
Cholula, boasting 365 churches around—at least one built on
the top of an Aztec temple—we stopped to look at two churches.
The first one we reached only after three or four miles on a dirt
road. Though rather unimpressive from outside, it had a fabulous
interior, every square inch carved and painted in brilliant colors!
The predominant features were rather life-like faces in intervals
along the columns. To Mr. Wasson, the predominant features
were some cherubs carrying mushrooms …

We ate lunch at Puebla, eating *mole*, an excruciating dish
consisting of chicken with a coffee and chocolate sauce, if
you can imagine that! Outside on the street they were playing
marimbas or instruments resembling xylophones, but sounding
like a tinny orchestra. From there we drove to Tehuacán to
spend the night.

The next day, we took the small plane for Huautla (pronounced
wowt-la). The flight is some twenty minutes in duration. The
landing field is a narrow strip along the top of a ridge. On
the approach, it didn't look as though the plane were going

to clear the steep cliff leading up to the start of the field. The country consists of endless green mountains, most of which are cultivated with maize—some mountains so steep that the Indians have to plant and harvest by aid of rope. Huautla is three miles from the landing strip.

The village is perched along the mountainside; the houses are mostly constructed of adobe with thatch and tin roofs. The streets are all mud and rock, with one lone stretch paved. As in all Mexican villages, it has a large square, two in fact— one for the market place and adjacent another square bordered by the church and the school. We stayed with Herlinda, a schoolteacher—or, rather, slept in an empty house across the street and ate at her house. Our house was blessed with a tin roof and plenty of rooms in which to store things. Beds were mysteriously produced for the three girls and Mr. Wasson. The only decoration was some old newspapers plastered on the wall and one or two posters.

The language in Huautla is Mazatec, a tonal language like Chinese, and very musical and pleasant to listen to. About half (or more than half) the Indians do not speak Spanish at all, but all the children presumably learn Spanish at school. The women dress very colorfully, especially on market day with rather shapeless long dresses with the most colorful designs. The men wear pants, shirts, always hats, and often serapes. The men, by the way, can whistle the language (the women are not allowed). These Indians are very short in stature, and though very cute as children, only a few of the women could be called handsome by our standards. They have—as do most Indians— wide mouths, high cheekbones, and black hair, usually braided.

Herlinda is an acculturated Indian—she married a white man (who deserted her), and her two sons live in Taluca, a town fifty kilometers west of Mexico City.

She is Mr. Wasson's mushroom agent, buying the hallucinatory mushrooms for thirty pesos and selling them for a hundred pesos per kilo to Smith, Kline & French (a pharmaceutical company) that is trying to determine the hallucinatory agent. When we arrived she had some sixty kilos of mushrooms; apparently this year was an exceptional one for the hallucinatory mushroom. Due to this great influx of wealth, she has a cook, and her family stays with her—three relatives—Berta (fourteen), Concha (thirteen), and Pio (twelve). Concha is a lovely girl, and Pio most engaging, though one would never guess his age to be over eight. These Indian kids have marvelous smiles, and we spend quite a lot of time playing volleyball, cards, and other games with them. The five-to-twelve-year-olds and older are usually seen carrying their younger brothers and sisters about, taking most tender care of them. Until the age of three or more, no pants are worn.

Sunday is market day at Huautla—people come from all the neighboring villages to hawk their wares. The result is a very colorful scene: vegetables of all sorts, chickens, turkeys, pigs, clothes, serapes, material for the mushroom rite, and shoes. The square is transformed from an expanse of mud—dirt—to white tents and great crowds of Indians, all in their Sunday best.

Our food was fair, and in deference to Mrs. Wasson (this is the Wassons' fourth visit to Huautla), tortillas, beans and peppers seldom appeared. Huautla has never seen an automobile! In fact, I never saw a wheel—it was all donkeys, mules, and Indians, some with enormous loads carried by a strap around their foreheads. Coffee is their main money crop; one of Herlinda's acculturated teacher friends joked with us as to how the hallucinatory mushroom was becoming Huautla's second industry, especially as the coffee crop was poor.

Taxco or Tehuacán—the market and the town

Huautla and Huautla's market square

More facts about Huautla: the town is about 5,500 feet in altitude; several stores sell a variety of products (general stores); the estimated population is five thousand. There is also a jail, and even the Mexican Army is present. While the market was in session they were drilling some Indian recruits, who were incapable of the simplest maneuvers. There is also a movie house. We saw a dreadful Mexican movie, and an American serial that was, if anything, worse. Even the Indians were unimpressed, only laughing when the movie made fun of a priest, and screaming when a girl performed a bump and grind dance.

There is a two-story municipal building. On our first day, we paid a visit to the *presidente*. His main item of excitement seemed to be the discovery of a new cave, to which they offered to accompany us, but which we never reached due to rain and our unexpected departure.

Although the Indians in this town seem most cheerful, there is a sinister threat somewhere, for there is a replica of Murder, Inc. here—people who can be hired to kill! We discovered from Herlinda that her brother-in-law had been killed by men hired by the *presidente* (we actually talked to his assistant, as he was absent); he suspected him of making time with his beautiful wife.

Herlinda's testimony apparently sent one of the assassins to jail—hence, she has enemies in town. Our curandera's son (a *curandero or curandera* is a healer or shaman), a half-wit, was murdered also. She apparently divined who the assassins were, through the mushroom. Although I did not see anyone drunk, apparently the Indians get very ugly when drunk, and occasionally shooting occurs.

We spent an afternoon walking down to their graveyards—a typically colorful Catholic graveyard, only without any inscriptions. Their funerals are lugubrious affairs with a loud, inept band playing indistinguishable music, and apparently great drinking occurs.

Joanie, Masha, et al. Herlinda and
company with drying mushrooms

The Sacred Mushroom Rite

Our main purpose here is to bring back hallucinatory mushrooms—at which we are eminently successful—and to record a successful séance with the mushroom (at which the holy ghost makes its appearance!). And it is on Sunday afternoon that we are informed that tonight is the night and that Joanie and I are to attend and eat the mushroom!

We walk about a mile to the house where the mushroom rite is to be held, carrying the tape recording equipment. The house is of the usual adobe style and has two floors, one below the level of the street, which could be reached via a trap door, or by walking down the hill. About eight thirty the curandera Maria Sabena appears, accompanied by some others, who later disappear. She must be fifty or so, rather slight, but holding herself very straight and conducting herself with great dignity.

The main feature of her dress is a large dark-colored shawl, which is always wrapped around her in one way or another. There were quite a few other people living in the house; people kept coming and going, but the central characters are a man and his wife with their four children and one on the way. The man and his wife speak Spanish, and thus formed a bridge of communication between the curandera and us. The Indians all sit around and talk as the night continues, often talking with Mr. Wasson about one thing or another. Mr. Wasson, Joanie, the man, and I have some coffee, and what conversation I could catch concerned the steel and glass buildings of New York. We then set up the microphones, and at about nine o'clock the children are put to bed. After some five trips to acquire incense and various other necessities for the rite, the ceremony begins.

We are in a rather large room with a dirt floor, with some straw mats, a large double bed where the family slept, and another cot. It turns out that only Joanie, the curandera, the ten-year-old daughter of the "family," and I are to eat the mushroom. The man sits on the cot near the curandera to give the refrain, as much of the ceremony vaguely resembles responsive reading. The altar consists of a table, upon which are placed three pictures—one of Christ, two of saints—and two candles.

The curandera prays over the mushrooms, passes them through the smoke of the incense, and then hands them to us in a cup. There are several kinds of hallucinatory mushrooms, all apparently giving the same effect. I consume eight pairs of a small variety, and one big pair—after twenty minutes had elapsed and nothing had happened. Joanie has approximately the same dosage, perhaps a little less. The room is in total darkness, save for a little reflected light from the room where Mr. Wasson is running the tape recorders.

The curandera starts to chant after half an hour or more has elapsed, occasionally pausing to converse in a staccato voice with the man—his name is Cayetano—conversing ritualistically. The curandera becomes a different person, no longer so dignified, but alive and vibrant—sometimes plaintive in her voice, sometimes demanding. She even laughs occasionally, and then she looks the part of a witch. The rhythm of the chant is occasionally quite complicated, sometimes combined with clapping—clapping

82

done with both sides of her hands—then flinging her hands into space to throw her arms into somewhat contorted positions. She quite often claps without singing (chanting), sometimes hitting her chest, and other times banging the flat of her hand on the floor—all this with a certain rhythm that demands attention (not boring at all).

Joanie is in trouble from the mushrooms, feeling completely "lost," and what visions she sees all seem to be "very unpleasant." They apparently didn't give me enough, as I have no visions and no effect, save that my eyes are dilated, and I am very much awake. Joanie is continually amazed at me being myself and has been holding on to my hand. She has been feeling very cold, then very hot—or has no feelings; she has no sensation of having feet, or in fact of being "Joanie" at all.

The chanting stopped for awhile, and Mr. Wasson came in with a flashlight—a most sobering effect with his calm, American voice. I told him that I had no visions and that Joanie was feeling delirious. When this information was conveyed to the curandera, *aguardiente* was passed to Joanie and me—perfectly foul liquor made from sugar cane. And when Joanie almost gagged, the curandera spat two great mouthfuls of the foul stuff into her face from a distance of some three or four feet! And then she did the same to me—a cold, fine, foul spray. I don't know why she did it, but afterward Joanie felt blissfully happy instead of feeling frightened and miserable. Joanie had also lost her perception of space and had been unable to see the ceiling for some time. When she spat the liquor at us, there was no feeling she despised us, and later she said that she spat to purify the effects of the mushroom.

In the background, the sleepy sounds of the three children would occasionally break through, and once or twice, the mother had to suckle the baby. As the ceremony went on, cigarettes were in great demand, and when I ran out (I smoked back then), the curandera brought out a great cigar to smoke. The little girl occasionally joined in the talk, usually during the breaks when the curandera wasn't praying or chanting. Quite often, one could distinguish Saint Peter, Saint Paul and Christ, in her chants. She would repeat the first three or four lines of the Lord's Prayer in Spanish—apparently these were the only Spanish words she knew.

After a while, around three in the morning, Mr. Wasson quit recording and went to bed, the curandera informing him that the séance, as such, was over. Cayetano went to bed with his family, and then ensued a long musical conversation between the curandera and the wife, with occasional grunts from Cayetano to provide the tenor voice for the trio. Occasionally, one would hear references to the saints, so I presume the talk was religious. The wife, in one soliloquy, went on for practically ten to fifteen minutes without a break.

At about four o'clock we all went to sleep, and at six we awakened, and the recording equipment was removed. Mr. Wasson informed the curendera that he had no money with him and that if she would drop by Herlinda's, he would pay her (which was just a ploy, as he did have the money). So the curendera appeared at Herlinda's, and a séance was arranged to take place at Herlinda's in two or three days. There were bad feeling between the curendera and Cayetano's household, as one of Cayetano's relatives was privy to the assassination of the curendera's half-wit son—this discovered through the divine mushroom.

The day after all this, Joanie, Masha, and I went for a walk. We climbed up a hill where we could see for miles—green mountains, mostly covered with maize stretching out into the distance. Joanie collected flowers, and I collected reptiles, as Dick Zweifel had given me some plastic bags and some formaldehyde. We found four or five frogs, two of them not any bigger than this dot (quarter inch round)—four lizards all of the same variety, and one small snake. I haven't been birding here—vultures are common, soaring regally in the sky, and I identified one grosbeak—all blue, with pink wing bars.

Another day, the day of the mushroom rite, Mr. Wasson and I walked up to the airfield to check on the mushrooms that were awaiting clear weather to be flown back. We met a Dr. Singer, an eminent mycologist (someone who studies fungi) and some assistants, who had come to collect the mushrooms for some foundation. Mr. Wasson's article,—"Seeking the Magic Mushroom," published in *Life Magazine* (in May 1957)—and his book had attracted a great number of scientists and curiosity seekers (to visit Huautla, that is). We met an American later who spoke not a word of Spanish, accompanied by a cheap Mexican interpreter, who exclaimed that he was interested in all religions, etc.

The divine mushroom, once never mentioned in public, is now commonly discussed and sold. However, it is doubtful Maria will ever be corrupted like the local officials were— officials who consider themselves soothsayers and who seem to have a monopoly, though probably most are fakes.

The only other honest curandera that the Wassons found was Aurelio, who divined for the Wassons that their son was in New York and about to go into the army—when he was supposed to be in Boston—and also that he had a girlfriend, etc. His séance was entirely different from Maria's, in that only Aurelio consumed the mushroom. Also, all sorts of props were involved—feathers, throwing of corn kernels, etc. Unlike Maria, he does not sing or chant, but his divinations turned out to be true!

On the credit side, the *Life* article has acquainted the

acculturated Indians such as Herlinda with the mushroom rite, and let them know that their village has something to be proud of, rather than ashamed of. Maria was at first very disturbed when she heard that her picture (in the article) was now public, but her friends assured her it was a great honor. When Mr. Wasson showed her the photographs, she was very happy with them. In one of them, Maria is talking to her half-wit son with a machete in the background that she had not noticed before. She decided it was supernatural, a sign that her son would be murdered.

After collecting my reptiles, I offered the Indian children one peso for frogs and lizards, and two for snakes. Seemingly every child in the village went collecting, and although I made my offer late one afternoon, the next day I had to lower my price to fifty centavos for frogs and one peso for lizards and snakes, and finally to twenty-five centavos for frogs and fifty centavos for lizards and snakes. I must have received seventy-five frogs of some ten varieties, forty lizards of three varieties, and ten snakes all the same species. When I tried to put a stop to it, it was like the broom scene in *Fantasia*—their faces were so tragic that I almost had to buy more!*

---

* N.B.: Photographs of Currendera Maria Sabina and her altar with Gordon Wasson added on page 123 with permission from Gordon Wasson Archives, Harvard University Herbaria & Libraries.

Second Séance with the curandera

The climax of our trip was the second séance with Maria Sabina at Herlinda's. Maria, her daughter (Apolonia), and four children all came for supper. The oldest child had learned Spanish at school, the only one of her family who could speak the language. The youngest child was still in the nursing stage, and another was on the way. The daughter is a curendera in her own right—Maria's father was also a curandero. We ate a simple supper—soup and bread, Mr. Wasson asking Maria about one thing or another. Herlinda is going to take the mushroom also—which is a long step for her, as two years ago she would not have touched it, believing stories about people committing violent acts under the influence. She is taking it for "scientific" purposes—not religious.

After supper, the curandera and her family all sat and/or stood together and talked to one another, in their soft, musical way. Maria is every inch the head of her family—dignified— very straight in posture. Her daughter is far earthier, blowing her nose in her shawl, suckling the baby, belching (in rhythm), etc.

Mr. Wasson had already set up the recording machines. At Mrs. Wasson's insistence, Masha is not taking the mushroom, and Joanie decided not to either. Thus, only Herlinda and I (aside from the two curanderas), are taking the mushroom. It's probably a good thing that Masha is going to help her father with the machines, as he goofed during the last séance and didn't record anything.

Around nine, the children started getting ready for bed. Masha offered them her cigarettes, and all the children save the baby had one. With great gaiety the children pulled their blankets around them and settled down in one corner of the room. Shortly afterward, the curandera starts praying in front of the altar and examining the mushrooms. I should have mentioned that various questions and problems are presented to the curendera to be answered by the Holy Ghost, who appears through the divine mushroom—questions about health, questions about relatives, and so forth. Mrs. Wasson asked about her health and her son—whether he would get married, etc.

Herlinda placed the incense burner next to her, and she passed the mushrooms through it; it wasn't long before the room was filled with incense. At approximately ten o'clock the mushrooms were presented to Herlinda and me. I ate six pairs of the larger variety called *Nishitot*,* and Herlinda, helped along by chocolates and *(encouraged by)* Mrs. Wasson, ate four pairs. These mushrooms are *not* delectable, gastronomically. At approximately ten forty-five, the lights were put out and the curandera began to chant, the daughter answering her staccato questions, in a whisper at first. For long periods, the curandera repeated the first few lines of the Lord's Prayer, the first line *"Padre Nuestro"* more often. Then she suddenly broke into her chant—a complicated rhythm to it, constantly changing, and

---

* G.W. refers to these mushrooms as *derrumbe* in his book The Wondrous Mushroom.

often a melody—and clapping while singing. Her daughter sang too, occasionally, but not a duet.

I thought this would be a repetition of the other night, for it wasn't until midnight that I really felt the power of the mushroom. I began to see Byzantium designs in all sorts of colors—the colors resembling those of a stained glass window—and the designs rushed by, one after another. The only thing I saw besides the designs was the face of a girl from some perfume advertisement, which was probably the result of my daydreaming that the mushroom would tell me what the girl I shall marry looks like. I sat and yawned—great, huge yawns—and grinned and grinned, for I felt ridiculously happy—in a state of euphoria.

But Herlinda felt nothing of the sort. The mushrooms sent her promptly to hell! The curandera gave her aguardiente and cigarettes—and she got drunk and sick! She told us later that she thought she was going to die! The constant refrain along with *Padre Nuestro* was "*más agua*" ("more water") from Herlinda, sending Masha and Joanie scurrying off and returning with glasses of water. About one in the morning she got sick to her stomach—seemingly endlessly. She finally disappeared from the scene for a while, praying in the corner and briefly sleeping with her children. Pio got frightened, and he was crying for his aunt when she went to bed with them (they had been moved out of the main room, and Masha had put her sleeping bag where they had been). Mrs. Wasson had left around twelve thirty. I was all wrapped up in my sleeping bag and managed to get into all sorts of upside down and other positions, especially while watching my visions.

I could have stopped the visions, but I didn't care to, and even with one's eyes open, they filled the screen. They ceased more or less around two. Smoking a cigarette becomes an entirely different sensation. As one's eyes are dilated, the cigarette and the glow of its ash seem akin to a cigar, and the smoke tastes—I have no adjective …

The curandera stops occasionally in her praying and chanting to smoke a cigarette; she shook my hand once or twice—a shock of communication when we touched. At the start of the evening she barely touched anyone, but at the end she really shook it. She called us all in at one point to say "Our Father" in our own languages. Herlinda came back after awhile—no longer sick—and she talked for a long time with the curandera's daughter. Even I could understand that they were calling the saints for Herlinda. The curandera examined me (this last part is all taking place in candlelight) by touching me in a strange way on my forehead and cheeks, saying through Herlinda that my thoughts were pure and saintly (Herlinda could speak English). She also felt my fingers and forearm—pulling my fingers, all with the quick, sure touch of an osteopath—and gave me a clean bill of health. She also said that she had been sick for all of us, that my finger was a passing thing (I had accidentally shot it with dust shot during the museum expedition), that Mrs. Wasson should get better, that Peter was in love with his girl now, but that he was a person who demanded too much, and she doubted they would be married.

I wrote a "poem" the next day and revised it a little later:

The Divine Mushroom

Padre Nuestro—Padre Nuestro—Padre Nuestro
The chant, a melody—the musical talk, the staccato chitchat;
Tobacco, aguardiente, incense, children sleeping in the corner;
The darkness, the rhythmical clapping, the handshake reaching across the abyss.
The Shaman erect, supernatural, gypsy, vibrant;

Her daughter Indian, impish, suckling her baby—the answering
voice—
And the mushroom and an indescribable feeling of bliss!

A shade was drawn across the trivia, the countless sidetracks,
worries and anger.
I am in a fairyland of rushing Byzantium designs in pinks and
purples and greens and reds;
A fairyland where all is in superlatives like Alice's Wonderland
or the City of Oz.
A fairyland or perhaps Heaven on Earth for words fail to describe
the feeling.
I shall never ever be so happy!

And toward the end I felt purged.
I was pure as a saint and one with God (if there is one),
And one with the primitive Shaman, who for all her sorcery,
earthly spitting, foul aguardiente,
Was next to Truth and so was I!

Joanie says she likes my poetic effort, and that she had felt
the same way when she ate the mushroom; not the visions so
much as the happy feeling and religious feeling. We all went to
sleep around four that morning, and I didn't wake till eight.

The curandera left early, as apparently her grandchild had
diarrhea all over her, this witnessed by Joanie. Mr. Wasson
made a terrific racket putting his equipment away and finally
went to the other house with Masha. He had found out that the
pilot refused to take the mushrooms, so he left for the airfield
at seven in the morning.

I don't think I was as physically affected by the mushroom as
Joanie was, or Masha two years ago, as I could see the ceiling,

could wiggle my toes, and felt something when I bit my finger. It was about two thirty in the morning when Herlinda came back. The three women were wrapped in shawls, all kneeling in the eerie candlelight, looking for all the world like Shakespeare, the daughter occasionally smiling at me in the most impish way.

For those who might look upon the mushroom as a "jag"—a narcotic, it might well be; if that's the effect heroin gives you, I'm surprised there aren't more dope addicts! There is no hangover with this, though. When I woke up, I still felt happy—though somewhat pooped.

We found out on Mr. Wasson's return that we are leaving tomorrow, for he feels that this is the only way to get the mushrooms out of Huautla. Masha, Joanie, and I tried to find the much talked about caves, but taking the wrong road, we ended up with a pleasant but exhausting two-hour hike up and down hills.

Mr. Wasson had an interview with the lady schoolteachers that afternoon, and, after asking him all about the mushrooms, their leader formally requested Mr. Wasson donate an outhouse for their school. Mr. Wasson, who is not slow on his feet, said he would have to discuss it with his wife. When we heard about this at supper, we demanded that he do so, that it was the least he could do for Huautla. He replied that he might if they named it after him.

So, laden with mushrooms and reptiles, we bid farewell to Huautla. Mrs. Wasson had treated Herlinda's cook's child, who probably had a fatal disease, and gave the family—the children—clothes. The woman had done her best to be our "maid," though not quite.

Return to Cuernavaca and Sightseeing

he flight back was pleasant—the best pilot. One of their best pilots, though, and his passenger, were killed landing at this airstrip, attempting to land from the mountainside rather than the cliffside, a tricky wind turning him over and throwing the plane into the abyss! We had arrived on a Friday and left on a Thursday, in all a most remarkable week.

We brought Herlinda back with us, and the next day Masha and I drove her to Toluca, where her two sons, and seemingly even more relatives than at Huautla, were congregated. In attempting to drive through the country rather than through Mexico City on our return, we ran into some terrible roads, and it took us three hours and forty-five minutes—an hour and a half longer. Spectacular country some of it, a plateau crisscrossed by canyons — cattle country.

The next weekend was spent swimming and playing tennis. The Wassons had some guests for Sunday lunch, and we listened to an American real estate man in Cuernavaca describe Mexican justice. One can literally get an injunction for a future murder, and a rich man is essentially free to do what he pleases, as long as he pays the proper people when he gets into trouble.

We listened to the tape recording of the séance that afternoon. It's very good in spots, but there is too much whispering, and one hears Herlinda begging for water too much. We had a long discussion about religion a few nights later. It is Joanie's and presumably Mr. Wasson's theory that religion started with—if not the hallucinatory mushroom—then something like it. To call the elements of nature supernatural is a long step, rather than simply to take them for granted. The whole structure of religion—the witch doctor, the sacrifice, the ceremonies— where and how did it all start? Primitive man eating the hallucinatory mushroom would certainly be the answer, for without the words *drug* or *hallucinatory* in one's vocabulary, the mushroom would be a great supernatural power—a God speaking and making himself and his power known through the mushroom!

Monday—no *Sunday*, Norbert LeRoy, a Morgan partner, and his French friend Armand arrived by plane. The next day, after lunch with an anthropologist who has accompanied the Wassons on several of their trips, we set forth to see the Cathedral of Guadalupe and Maximilian's palace. The cathedral is a shrine, erected on the spot where a Mexican Indian saw a vision of the Virgin Mary. The Mexicans who enter the cathedral do so on their knees. The church is sinking at one end, the chandeliers forming an angle of at least three degrees with the pillars.

Maximilian's castle is a fine castle built high on a hill, thus affording an excellent view of Mexico City, and two snow-capped volcanoes beyond. Norbert led all save Mrs. Wasson up a workman's ladder to the top level (they are repairing the castle) to find an even better, if unlawful view. One can imagine a beautiful full dress ball here as the gardens are spacious, and located so that all of Mexico City is visible.

Tuesday we set out to see a Toltec (Mayan) temple—some three-quarter hour drive from here. We drove about three and a half kilometers up a dirt and rock road and walked another kilometer or less up to the top of the hill. From the various mounds, one excavated house, and some *pelota* (ball) courts, one can imagine the ancient Toltec village, a village of priests, as I understand it. The pyramid we came to see had been excavated and restored in places. As with most Mexican pyramids, it is truncated, with stairs leading up one side to the platform on top, which at one time presumably had a temple built on top of it. Along the sides are some bas-reliefs carved in the rock—dragons with great teeth and tongues, with fire coming out of their nostrils—and jaguars, men, designs, eagles, etc. From the top, one can see for miles in all directions—long ranges of mountains and plains. On the way back we had cocktails at a very fashionable hotel (with modern architecture) by a lake. The car boiled over, but apparently without damage.

The following day, Thursday, July 25, we set out in the afternoon to see the Pyramid of the Sun and the Pyramid of the Moon. They are most impressive, the Pyramid of the Sun rising to over two hundred feet—with steps leading up one side and a platform on the top. This was where many Aztecs perished in the sacrificial rites. Standing on the summit one can see for miles around, a considerable area consisting of ruins of Aztec houses, and other temples, including the Pyramid of the Moon, which is similar but smaller. We also saw the great court where thousands once stood to hear the pronouncements of the priests and the king. There are several pyramids here, including one that dates back to approximately AD 400, with magnificent, sculptured dragons emerging from the wall of the pyramid. The Aztec pyramids were built much later—they had no sculpture or bas-relief, but were covered with frescoes.

Toltec Temple—close-up and view (camera damaged)

We also looked at some frescoes inside what was once, presumably, a priest's house. The fresco depicted drowned men in their particular heaven—where they could do as they pleased. To represent their talkativeness, great curlicues emanated from their mouths, slightly reminiscent of comic strips. Mr. Wasson, of course, has found some mushrooms depicted here and has this fresco and another, which we peeked through bars to see, reproduced in his book.

Friday, everyone save Mr. Wasson, Joanie, and I left on Norbert's plane for Guadalajara to spend a few days. Joanie will drive to Tucson, Arizona, with me, and we plan to stop there on our way. I finally beat the pro in tennis. Spent the afternoon playing bridge with Joanie, and reading *The Pearl* by John Steinbeck, a neat story. The crowd is back, having journeyed to Taxco, but the weather was too bad to fly.

Saturday we traveled to "Mexico" and Valle de Bravo with Professor Weitlaner, the anthropologist who introduced the Wassons to Herlinda and Huautla. The generator of the Ford was on the blink, and we only got the car fifteen minutes after the time set for departure. I should perhaps backtrack to mention that on Friday, Joanie, Masha, and I traveled to Amecameca and some beautiful watering spas. The road led through some rather impressive canyons and villages. Joanie had misread the guidebook, so we expected to find Aztec ruins at Amecameca, but *no.* We walked up a hill and viewed a church overlooking the valley. On the way back, we had tea at a German restaurant.

Exploring Elsewhere for the Mushroom

B ack to Saturday—we picked up Don Roberto Weitlaner at approximately two in the afternoon, and set forth across the mountains to Toluca, and from there to an Indian town near Tenango, where Don Roberto had some contact with a curandera—we hoped to obtain the hallucinatory mushroom used in this area. The country is fertile—miles of maize. Our village, as Tenango, is perched on the side of a hill—with thatched and red tile roofs—and a panorama of other villages and wooded hills across the valley, and mountains in the distance.

We failed to obtain the mushroom, so we headed for Valle de Bravo—an hour plus drive from Toluca down a road without one straight stretch. As we approached Valle de Bravo, about the same altitude as Cuernavaca, we entered a magnificent pine forest. Valle de Bravo is an old Indian town with cobblestone streets on the shores of a man-made lake. We were given directions to an inn four miles from town.

On arriving, we found an almost Swiss chalet set in a pine forest with a rushing waterfall alongside it, and a most modern Swiss-style inn. Over some mescal, we discussed anthropology—Don Roberto told us about age grouping in the Chinatec Indians.

He is a most delightful old man—he's seventy-two—who spent the last thirty or forty years in Mexico, three months out of every year spent in the Indian country. He is now writing a tome on the Chinatec Indians. We had an excellent supper—the Lions Club of Valle Bravo congregating, as we were finishing, some one hundred strong.

Our program is to visit various Sunday markets to find anyone who knows about the hallucinatory mushroom. Valle de Bravo was the first market we visited, Don Roberto and Mr. Wasson wending their way to the mushroom vendors—but no success here. We drove back up the road to Toluca, stopping about halfway at another Indian village. Joanie and I wandered around watching the market, while the two men hunted for mushrooms; Don Roberto was often seen squatting with some ancient Indian. Joanie bought some shawls, and we saw a medicine man selling feathers, herbs, etc., to ward off disease. Nothing here either, so we journeyed on to Toluca, stopping by Herlinda's house to say hello, and hearing about the earthquake in Mexico City. Don Roberto and Mr. Wasson had felt it at Valle de Bravo, while both Joanie and I had slept through it.

Our next stop was Tenango, a huge market stretching in all directions, the Indians selling everything under the sun. Mr. Wasson found himself one mushroom here, with a promise of more the following Sunday. Joanie and I climbed halfway up the hill looking out over the valley and got caught in various people's back yards on our way down, begging our pardon right and left—*con permisso*.

We left about two thirty in the afternoon, arriving in Mexico City about three thirty. We did not see any of the damage (from the earthquake)—Don Roberto's house was untouched. There we found a telegram from one of Don Roberto's pupils who was going to go with us to Sochiapan in the Chinantla—land of the Chinatec Indians, so tomorrow we leave to look for more mushrooms.

On Monday, Norbert LeRoy flew us to Tehuacán. He has a Bonanza, a lovely plane. Mexico's three volcanoes were visible, the snow cones glistening in the sun.* We reached Tehuacán just in time to catch the train—we could see it chugging along as we landed. We took the train from Tehuacán to Cuicaltán. The tracks curve and curve again along a flat plain—the builders obviously paid by the kilometer. We sat in a first class coach. Mr. Wasson met a man he had known as the tax collector in Huautla three years before—they exchanged great, effusive greetings. Cuicatlán is in the hot country—the land is mostly cultivated, with bare mountains rising to form a river valley. We met Roberto Escalante, our guide, at the station. We spent most of the afternoon (we arrived at two thirty) getting mules and horses for the next day's journey. This always involved having a long talk with the *presidente*. This one seemed fairly influential; we got the animals.

Tuesday: we left about nine in the morning. The trail goes straight up, seemingly, two thousand feet or so. The country is semiarid with an abundance of organ cactus, a blue green cactus perhaps resembling an organ. We reached our destination, Concepción Pápalo, at approximately two thirty that afternoon. Cuicatlán is 1,500 feet; Pápalo is 6,500–7,000 feet.

Upon arrival we immediately worried about animals for the next day. The *presidente* didn't show up until six in the evening, though. Mr. Wasson presented him with a copy of some old Spanish histories of the town, which were read with great interest by his entire staff, secretaries, etc. They all read it aloud.

During the afternoon we visited the bell tower, one bell

---

* *Popocatepeti, Izlaccihauti and Citlaltepeti*

dating back to the 1700s. We also heard the schoolchildren sing the national anthem in incredible discord. We ate with the family who owns the store, in the usual thatched hut, the two women making tortillas—as women did two thousand years ago, rolling the dough on a stone board (*metate*), patting them, and baking them over an open fire.

We slept in the municipality. We awoke the next morning to find the promised animals two days away. After endless talking and messengers being sent in every direction, they arrived about eleven in the morning. Pápalo is not a Chinatec town; we were warned with greatest solemnity of the dangerous voyage ahead and of the terrors of Chinantla.

Our destination is Tecomaltianguisco, an eight-hour trip. We rode and walked uphill most of the morning, reaching a height of about eleven thousand feet. On the descent, we walked through a magnificent, moist forest with great pines and deciduous trees reaching far into the sky, with little undergrowth. Mushrooms were very common, including a lovely red variety. Later in the afternoon we descended further, coming into a rain forest—dense foliage, all sorts of moss, and other parasites growing on the trees. The slope was much steeper here—we walked down the steep slope seemingly endlessly. The weather was foggy, but occasionally the sun would break through, and one would suddenly be presented with a vista of mountainous, jungle-like terrain—the river valley far below.

Suddenly, the rain forest gave way to corn, and we were in Tecomaltianguisco. The *presidente* and his staff were all drunk, and were most unfriendly. But Mr. Wasson presented some letters, and we were permitted to sleep in the schoolhouse. We fortunately met the schoolmaster, who gave us supper. Mr. Wasson and Roberto went to see Professor W's compadre—he had been made compadre or Godfather of a girl on one of his trips though the town. This relationship is important in these towns—all sorts of gifts are presented, and the first compadre may have to give a fete for his godson.

We obtained a mule from the schoolmaster and started out the next morning for Sautla—one hour downhill—where he teaches. Mr. Wasson decided to get another mule to ride for the three-hour trip mostly uphill for San Pedro Sochiapan, our final destination. School was postponed as we sat talking with the *maestro* (teacher) waiting for the mule. This is a Chinatec town, and the maestro doesn't speak Chinatec. While we were waiting, he demonstrated his skills with two Indian boys. They would sit, stand, and fetch a stick in Spanish, and they knew the words for the parts of the body and certain other things, but they had a difficult time pronouncing the Spanish words.

Mr. Wasson's mule finally arrived and we set out for Sochiapan. After some twenty minutes downhill, we reached the river, a rushing mountain torrent spanned by a hammock bridge. We promptly went swimming while our porters carried the luggage across.

The mules were pulled across via a long rope—stumbling and splashing across. The deepest part is about four feet deep or less. The bridge is made from vines—two large braids—six inches in diameter, laid across with single or double vines supporting the canes every two or three feet.

The remaining walk to Sochiapan is steeply uphill for two hours. Mr. Wasson's mule misjudged his footing in a mud hole and toppled over rather slowly, landing himself and Mr. Wasson unceremoniously in the mud. Fortunately, he didn't roll, so no one was hurt.

We are greeted at Sochiapan by the *presidente* and a considerable crowd, and also with some fermented sugar cane, a great improvement on aguardiente. We are to sleep in the downstairs office—his house is in the municipality, where there

Mr. Wasson and the mules. Crossing the river!

is a store and other buildings. Sochiapan, like all of these towns, has a church and a jail, and they are building a municipality building. The church has an enormous thatched roof over it. There is also a school building and a basketball court. There must be between 500 and 750 living in the village. From our open door we can see range after range of green mountains—some cultivated with milpas—corn patches, and other wild forest. Sochiapan must be five- or six-thousand feet in elevation. Mr. Wasson told the *presidente* about our purpose in visiting his town, and he has promised to send out his agents in search of it. The food here is the same as in other towns—beans, tortillas, eggs, and occasionally chicken soup (with the chicken it it), and baked bananas.

Friday was spent talking to various informants that Roberto knows, talking to the maestro, etc. There are only about fifteen people in the village who speak Spanish. I went for a walk in the morning—the country is mostly cultivated, save for strips of tangled rain forest where the big streams come down the mountainside. There is an abundance of tropical butterflies—a lot resembling those we caught in Ecuador, including the great blue Morpho.* Birds are not so commonly seen, save for the ever-present vultures. I saw one lovely brown pigeon-like bird fly up.

The study of anthropology must be most interesting, for these Indian towns are different worlds from ours. For instance, the idea of germs causing disease is entirely foreign to them—it is always some evil spirit, or some person putting a hex on them.

---

* At age thirteen (1946), I got to travel to Ecuador with my family, and we spent time with a naturalist in the jungles there. I collected butterflies for my sister Sarah, who stayed at home. The naturalist, Dean Hobbs Blanchard, wrote a book about his travels entitled *Ecuador: Crown Jewel of the Andes*, (Vintage Press 1962).

Thus, they call the curandero to intercede for them. Prayers are given to Christian saints, the thunder and lightening, dead elders, and others. I talked later with an American missionary, a linguist and anthropologist, who is writing a paper with Professor W. on age grading—his tribe being the Miche, Professor W's being the Chinatec.

The evangelist missionaries, having for the most part failed to convert the Indian, have turned their zeal to linguistics and have produced some of the foremost linguists in the world. Missionaries in Huautla have translated Mr. Wasson's tape recordings.

The Miche and the Chinatec have very similar age gradings, and being entirely separate in their languages, this leads Professor W. to believe that this is a very fundamental age grouping. From the various groups—age groups—come the various functionaries of the municipality and the church. In the Miche town described, everyone becomes *president*, regardless of ability, for one year. Roberto doesn't think there is age grouping in this town, but there certainly is a large court around the *presidente*. Some are teenagers; in age grouping, first the boys work for the church and later run errands for the municipality. In Sochiapan, there is a heap of stones and some crosses which form a dividing line of the town—one has to marry across the line.

The American missionary I mentioned earlier described some of the difficulties in moving into an Indian town cold. He discovered later, after getting to know them, that all sorts of terrible stories were circulated as to his presence—stealing babies, hunting sacred animals, etc. He speaks Miche perfectly, and his wife speaks Miche and another Indian language. These languages are incredibly difficult—involving tones, glottal stops, different lengths of sounds, etc. There are some fifty entirely distinct languages in Mexico, without any relationship between them. The Chinatecs, the Miches, the Zapotecs, and the Mazatecs—all are in adjoining towns, and all speak languages apparently as different from one another as from English! Chinatec is a monosyllabic language—almost every word having just one syllable. This makes for rather explosive sounds; though tonal, it has none of the music of the Mazatec.

We found that the mushroom is eaten only by the curandera or curandero and that only one person is present at the séance. From the descriptions we heard, the séance usually has to do with a stolen machete or stolen money, and apparently the mushroom always uncovered the mystery. The agents all come back from the long day in the woods without the mushroom.

I watched the children (teens) play basketball, and my, what fun they had! For two hours or more, they played furiously— and if two struggled over the ball, another from either team would take the ball and throw it up for a jump ball. The game was played in both Chinatec and Spanish—the maestro playing for half of the game.

The *presidente* speaks only Spanish. He is the doctor, the distiller, owner of mules, horses, pigs, turkeys, chickens and dogs; he supports the blind, runs the store, etc. There is a blind Indian who clings to a post all day!

Tomorrow we go to Santiago Quetzalapa to see a half-Indian half-Frenchman (he speaks Spanish and Chinatec) about the divine mushroom. A year and a half ago he was the Presidente of Sochiapan, but journeying from Cuicatlán with four others, the four ate a mushroom and three of them died. He didn't eat the mushroom and so was chased out of town.

There was a lovely sunset that evening—a great, huge, pink thundercloud sending down torrents of rain and lightning on a mountain valley perhaps ten miles distant.

Basketball. Mountain town

Mr. Wasson bargaining, and with townspeople

Santiago Quetzalapa is on the river, some two thousand feet lower than Sochiapan. The Frenchman was not there when we arrived, so we explored the village. In four or five houses we found people weaving the *huipiles*, the shapeless but beautiful garment the women wear. In one house, the old woman wove several of them. It is all done by hand—there must be fifty strings in the "frame*" with some ten instruments crossing the frame—a very complicated looking procedure. She has the design in her head. Her granddaughter was spinning the wool outdoors.

The Frenchman came about one thirty in the afternoon. He informed us that the mushroom we were after was out of season, but that he would dry some and send them to Mr. Wasson. From the description, which included a carrion smell, Mr. Wasson thinks he already knows the mushroom—a rare variety that apparently also grows in Maine.

On the way back, we took a second swim in the river (we had taken a dip on the way there)—this time accompanied by some modest Indian boys. They were having a fine time shouting and leaping into the swift current. I say "modest" as they would hold their hands over their private parts when standing on the rocks. There was a tropical forest along the banks with all sorts of tropical butterflies flying about.

Upon our return we found out the *presidente's* agents and our informant had been unsuccessful in their hunt for the mushroom. I have neglected to mention that the Frenchman told us of going to a curandera twice, once over a stolen machete and once over stolen money, and that both times the curandera discovered their whereabouts through the divine mushroom.

We decided to leave Sunday morning for a ranch less than a two-hour journey from Teotila, where there is an airstrip that

---

*   known as a backstrap loom

Roelio, the same man who flies to Huautla, flies to. We visited the church before leaving—inside it is similar to any other. We had a grand meal of pork for breakfast. They had killed a pig the day before—and not very professionally. We had had pork fat for Saturday dinner, apparently considered delectable by the Mexican.

Sunday is the great drinking day in these Indian towns. They go to church at about seven o'clock, and the rest of the day seems to be devoted to consuming aguardiente. We watched the town council in action before we left, hearing the complaint of some Indian woman who was claiming that her neighbor was trying to throttle-choke her. After a long discourse, the woman finally left—apparently dismissed. I imagine justice is a little spotty up in this country—they had a seven-year-old boy in jail; he had accidentally killed a man with a shotgun—and they were sending him to Cuicatlán!

I only collected one frog here (or toad); Mr. Wasson told the *presidente's* sons that I would pay for specimens, but apparently they thought he was joking; when we returned from visiting the Frenchman, Mr. Wasson asked them about it, and great laughter ensued. We were given a great send-off with seemingly half the male population of the town there to see us off. Mr. Wasson and Roberto had mules.

I decided to walk it—a six-hour walk.

Upon arriving at the river, we found the entire (male) town of Zautla out repairing the bridge with much gesticulation and shouting. They were laying the vines across—putting better cane on the footpath, and generally attempting to strengthen it. The secretary explained that the bridge was very weak, and after we crossed it on Thursday, they decided it had to be strengthened.

After the river, we walked uphill for three straight hours—save for perhaps twenty minutes. We finally reached the ranch at about four thirty in the afternoon and discovered to our surprise that the rancher had an airstrip and two planes! He had some lovely Brahmin bulls that we walked by as we approached his ranch.

Swimming in the river. Repairing the bridge across it!

The rancher is a Spaniard—a very cordial, polite man who took us right in—gave us beds, etc. (We *did* have a letter from the Presidente of Sochiapan.) His house had windows, floors, etc., but as usual, we had beans and tortillas for supper. They are all evangelists in this country. Mr. Wasson listened to a conversation between the Indians and the rancher as to the battle between the evangelists and the Catholics concerning baptism—that the mature baptism was the way Christ was baptized—and that it was plainly obvious as to who was right. The rancher had hired his own schoolteacher. He also owns two planes and has hired a pilot. He offered us his plane for transportation to Tehuacán. As he had been so hospitable we couldn't very well ask for mules to take us to Teotila, so we accepted.

We had supper with his maestro and foreman, both with great horizontal moustaches. An interminable grace was said before dinner by all three, and not in unison. His wife served us supper; he has six sons and daughters—two of whom were in Mexico City being educated.

Return to the States through
Guadalajara and Mazatlán

W e set forth at the very crack of dawn, flying in a
piper cub big enough for two people. Mr. Wasson
and I took the first voyage—I was squeezed into a
fetal position behind the second seat. We arrived safely—it was
a beautiful day with no wind. We found out from Robelio that
our pilot had had only thirty-five hours of flying time. We then
flew with Librado, Robelio's second pilot, to Mexico City, and
Frank, Mrs. Wasson and Joanie met us there. Cuernavaca and
food seemed a great luxury. Mrs. Wasson, Joanie, Norbert, and
Armand had spent several days in Oaxaca seeing the ruins of
Monte Alban etc.

Spent a day in Mexico City shopping, etc., and Wednesday,
Joanie and I bid farewell to Casa Mañana, and with every inch
of luggage space filled, set out for Patzcuaro, Guadalajara,
Mazatlán, Guaymas, and Portal, Arizona.

Patzcuaro is about a six- or seven-hour drive from Cuernavaca.
We stopped to peer in at a folk art museum in Toluca and an
archeological museum in Morelia. We found Patzcuaro, despite
much praise from the Wassons, guidebooks, etc., to be a dirty
tourist-ridden town. The tourists aren't as bad as the people who
prey on them, at least to us. We stayed at a cheap hotel. We took

a boat out into the lake to see the much-heralded Indian village on an island. The lake itself is fairly large—with a panorama of red-roofed towns and mountains for scenery. These Indians are Tarascan and amazingly still speak their own language and still fish in the old way despite (or because of) the wave of tourists and an enormous statue of someone on the top of their island.

Tarascan fishermen

They put on a display of their butterfly fishing nets for us out in the lake. They were there just for the tourists, and they collected a tip. I rather liked the island, though—I don't see how they could continue with their old customs—people were weaving and repairing some of their nets—with tourists plying about.

Guadalajara was our next stop. It is a rather beautiful city with great avenues and large plazas with fountains and flowers. We visited their cathedral, which, as most, is far more impressive outside than inside. Everything else we found closed, and no cockfights were scheduled for Thursday night. We were going to go to a soccer game, but it rained.

The next day we went shopping and visited a museum with some Murillo paintings (awful) and some Indian relics. We found nothing shopping—we even visited the glass factory and a suburb where the Indians are supposed to paint wonderful things on pottery—but we found them painting Chinese dragons on huge vases—good, but the Chinese are better.

Mazatlán next—some tropical forest, but the land is mostly cultivated. We stayed at La Siesta, the same hotel as visited on my Baja California expedition. The Pacific Ocean though had changed *(since my Baja expedition)*, and great rollers were sending clouds of spume off the rocky coast. We had a great time swimming at the beach opposite the hotel—several times I got ground into the sand bottom.

After another swim, we set off early for Guaymas, traveling mostly through desert and on a straight road, a rarity in Mexico. Of interest were some river crossings—several on railroad bridges and one across a concrete ford in two feet of flowing water—no brakes for ten miles as a result. We ate a picnic lunch in the desert—it was in bloom—green, with quite a few flowers.

At Guaymas, we stayed at a motel next to the Guaymas Inn, where we ate not far from San Carlos Bay on the Baja trip—we got lost on the way, driving some forty miles extra.

At a very early hour indeed we set forth for Portal (Arizona) and customs. I ended up pushing the car through customs as it was very hot—we were given no trouble at all, even though they caught Joanie trying to smuggle out some flowers she had pressed in, of all things, a book of Russian poetry—Pushkin.

We changed Joanie's ticket to a tourist flight to New York.

We stopped for lunch in Bisbee, Arizona, and discovered that Harrison M. Lavender was not buried in the Lavender Pit (also its color), but in a grave. We arrived in Portal about five in the evening to find Sarah, and everything was about the same, only there were more people (I had driven through on the way).

I am now at the Fort Union Ranch in New Mexico, staying with the Marshalls (cousins). We (Sarah and I) plan to spend some time with the Davis cousins in Nashville on the way back, but I have writer's cramp and can't possibly continue!

Commentary — Notes

MYSELF: I did enter law school that fall (September, 1957); see Notes at the end of the Baja Expedition journal. I never partook of the sacred mushroom again and never became too attracted to drugs—smoking marijuana making me too hungry, for instance. I did suffer once from consuming marijuana brownies, a lot stronger than smoking, essentially a bad trip. And my one try with LSD likewise ended up with a bad trip—had to ask for help from friends. Long since have I stopped smoking, and now it's a glass of wine and, once in a while, a bottle of beer.

MAP: iUniverse, my self-publisher, suggested I provide a map for my Journal. But even Google maps are not free, and are copy-righted. I thought to make my own map from one published in Gordon Wasson's book *The Wondrous Mushroom* (also copyrighted) — but then most of the towns we visited are not on that map, and many of them are too small to be found on any maps. Suffice it to say Huautla is located in the vast hilly rural countryside south of Mexico City, west of Veracruz, and north of Oaxaca. There is a road to Huautla now, and its population was approximately 32,000 in 2005, (5,000 in 1957). You can look up Huautla on Google; most of the towns we visited also have Wikipedia entries.

MUSHROOM: The Internet now provides instant access to the secrets of the Sacred Mushroom. You can read the June 1957 article in Life Magazine with photographs of the ceremony with curandera Maria Sabena *(Eva Mendez)* by Gordon Wasson. Wikipedia has articles about Gordon Wasson and the mushroom as well. Albert Hofmann, the chemist, did succeed in synthesizing the psychoactive compounds in the mushroom, now well known as *Psilocybin.* In 1962 Albert Hofmann brought along the psilocybin pills for Maria Sabina, and she reported through an interpreter that there was little difference between the pill and the mushroom. Now she would be able to serve people even when no mushrooms were available.

Timothy Leary and his associates Ralph Metzner and Richard Alpert *(Ram Dass)* conducted experiments at Harvard, and some studies such as the Concord Prison Experiment suggested promising results using psilocybin in clinical psychiatry. Their withdrawal from Harvard and advocacy of the hallucinogen spread the word. The Life article and subsequent publicity brought many people to Huautla — beatniks, hippies, serious researchers, even tour groups! Guest houses were put up for mushroom seekers. Apparently such rock stars as Bob Dylan, John Lennon, Mick Jagger and Keith Richards took pilgrimages to Huautla. Also the attention brought unwanted publicity, the Mexican police (selling drugs), and it was reported that Maria Sabena's house was burned down. Serious practitioners felt the recreational use of the sacred mushroom profaned it. One advantage to the halucinatory mushroom as a "drug" is that it is not habit forming, though little mention is made in the literature of the possibility of a "bad" trip!

Gordon Wasson defended his publicizing of the mushroom. "Had we refrained from presenting the facts as we knew them to be, a novel and I think a major chapter in Early Man's cultural history, not only in Mexico, would have perhaps vanished unnoticed."[*]

As noted in my Journal, "On the credit side the Life article has acquainted the acculturated Indians such as Herlinda with the mushroom rite and let them know that their village has something to be proud of rather than ashamed of. Maria was at first very disturbed when she heard that her picture (in the article) was now public, but her friends assured her it was a great honor. When Mr. Wasson showed her the photographs she was very happy with them. In one of them Maria is talking to her half-wit son with a machete in the background which she had not noticed before. She decided it was supernatural, a sign her son would be murdered."

Some definitions of interest copied from the prelude of *The Wondrous Mushroom:* "Mycolatry: Worship of a mushroom, specifically worship of entheogenic mushroom species in proto and prehistory as a means for communicating in grave circumstances with the Almighty Powers."

"Entheogen: 'God within us' — 'those plant substances that, when ingested, give one a divine experience, in the past commonly known as 'hallucinogens', 'psychedelics', etc. to each of which serious objections can be made. A group headed by the Greek scholar Carl A. P. Ruck advances 'entheogen' as fully filling the need, notably catching the rich cultural resonances evoked by the substances, many of them fungal, over vast areas of the world in proto and prehistory."

Gordon Wasson was a prolific writer, many of his books printed in fine and limited editions. See list of his articles

---

[*] *The Wondrous Mushroom Mycolatry in Mesoamerica,* R. Gordon Wasson, McGraw Hill, 1980, Prelude p. xvi — reprint edition to be available April 2013.

and books at the end of "Notes". One of his collaborators and consultants was Professor Richard Evans Schultes of Harvard, a long time director of the Botanical Museum. In fact it was Dr. Shultes' article in a 1938 edition of the Botanical Leaflets that alerted Gordon Wasson (and others) to the existence of the sacred mushroom, long denied by prior observers. Dr. Schultes was a student of Oakes Ames,* and the story goes that when he came to write his thesis on Peyote, Professor Ames told him that he should not spend his time in a Library, but instead experience the primary source directly. So student Schultes, who had never been west of the Hudson River, set forth for Oklahoma and elsewhere. And during the War and postwar as well he spent twelve years in the Amazon jungles of Columbia for botanical research (rubber trees resistant to disease), learning various native languages and researching entheogen plants as well. A list of Dr. Schultes's writings follows Mr. Wasson's. . . .

Selected articles and books by R. Gordon Wasson

Riedlinger, Thomas J. *The Sacred Mushroom Seeker: Essays for R. Gordon Wasson*. Portland: Dioscorides Press, 1990.

Wasson, R. Gordon, Stella Kramrisch, Jonathan Ott, and Carl A. P. Ruck. *Persephone's Quest: Entheogens and the Origins of Religion*. New Haven: Yale University Press, 1986.

Wasson, R. Gordon. *The Last Meal of the Buddha*. Journal of the American Oriental Society, Vol. 102, No. 4. (Oct. - Dec., 1982). p 591-603.

---

* My grandfather. See *Oakes Ames — Jottings of a Harvard Botanist*, Collected and edited by Pauline Ames Plimpton, Foreword by George Plimpton, Harvard Press, 1979.

Wasson, R. Gordon. *The Wondrous Mushroom: Mycolatry in Mesoamerica*. New York: McGraw-Hill, 1980. (Reprint by City Lights, 2012.)

Wasson, R. Gordon, et al. *The Road to Eleusis: Unveiling the Secret of the Mysteries*. New York: Harcourt, 1978.

Wasson, R. Gordon. *Maria Sabina and Her Mazatec Mushroom Velada*. N. Y. : Harcourt, 1976.

Wasson, R. Gordon. *A Review of Carlos Castaneda's "Tales of Power."* Economic Botany. vol. 28(3):245-246, 1974.

Wasson, R. Gordon. A *Review of Carlos Castaneda's "Journey to Ixtlan: The Lessons of Don Juan."* Economic Botany. vol. 27(1):151-152, 1973.

Wasson, R. Gordon. *A Review of Carlos Castaneda's "A Separate Reality: Further Conversations with Don Juan."* Economic Botany. vol. 26(1):98-99. 1972.

Wasson, R. Gordon. *A Review of Carlos Castaneda's "The Teachings of Don Juan: A Yaqui Way of Knowledge."* Economic Botany. vol. 23(2):197. 1969.

Wasson, R. Gordon. *Soma: Divine Mushroom of Immortality.* 1968.

Wasson, Valentina Pavlovna, and R. Gordon Wasson. Mushrooms, Russia and History. 1957.

Wasson, R. Gordon. Seeking the Magic Mushroom Life magazine, May 13, 1957

Selected Books by Dr. Richard Evans Schultes

Schultes, Richard Evans (1976). *Hallucinogenic Plants.* illus. Elmer W. Smith. New York: Golden Press.

Schultes, Richard Evans; and Albert Hofmann (1979). *Plants of the Gods: Origins of Hallucinogenic Use.* New York: McGraw-Hill.

Schultes, Richard Evans; and Albert Hofmann (1980). *The Botany and Chemistry of Hallucinogens* (2nd ed. ed.). Springfield, Ill.: Thomas.

Schultes, Richard Evans; and William A. Davis, with Hillel Burger (1982). *The* Glass Flowers *at Harvard.* New York: Dutton.

Schultes, Richard Evans (1988). *Where the Gods Reign: Plants and Peoples of the Colombian Amazon.* Oracle, Ariz.: Synergetic Press.

Schultes, Richard Evans; and Robert F. Raffauf (1990). *The Healing Forest: Medicinal and Toxic Plants of the Northwest Amazonia.* Portland, Or.: Dioscorides Press.

Schultes, Richard Evans; and Robert F. Raffauf (1992). *Vine of the Soul: Medicine Men, Their Plants and Rituals in the Colombian Amazonia.* Oracle, Ariz.: Synergetic Press.

Schultes, Richard Evans; and Siri von Reis (eds.) (1995). *Ethnobotany: Evolution of a Discipline.* Portland, Or.: Dioscorides Press.

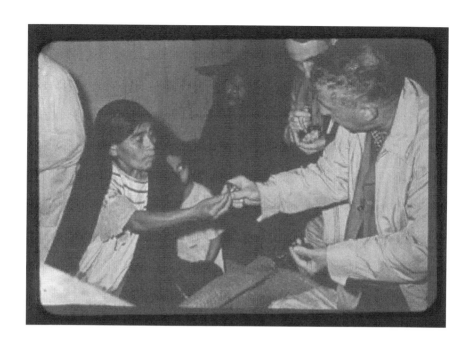

Currendera Maria Sabina handing the sacred mushroom to
Gordon Wasson; the altar before which she prays and chants.

45961852R00075

Made in the USA
San Bernardino, CA
22 February 2017